THE BIBLICAL TRUTH OF DA VINCI & GOD... *Encoded*

Miriam Parsons de Hostos

Blessings to you always
Miriam Parsons de Hostos

ISBN # 0-9785813-0-X

Title:
The Biblical Truth of Da Vinci & God...*Encoded*

Copyright 2006
Library of Congress
Control Number: 2006908399

by Miriam Parsons de Hostos

All rights reserved. Except for use in any review and excluding all Biblical scriptures, established scientific data, and pre-existing Da Vinci inter-net docs. The reproduction or utilization of this work in whole or in part in any form by any electronic, mechanical or other means, now known or hereafter invented, including recording or in any information storage or retrieval system, or for any scientific theory or discovery probe, Art, cinematic or Renaissance documentaries and classroom curriculums and theory, is forbidden without the written permission of the author.

Printed in the United States by Morris Publishing
3212 East Highway 30
Kearney, NE 68847
1-800-650-7888

For my mother,

Juana Bautista Torres Reyes de Hostos

&
Michael Anthony
Melissa Rae
Isaiah

Preface

Holy Bible: Psalm 90:10

………The days of our years are threescore years and ten; and if by reason of strength they be fourscore years, <u>yet</u> is their strength labour and sorrow; for it is soon cut off, and we fly away.

Hence, the genius and Master Artist Leonardo da Vinci lived to the age of 67 years old, close to the Bible parallels of 70 years to 80 years of mankind's expectancy of life on the earth; and quality thereof.

<u>Blessings and Curses</u>

Although Da Vinci was spiritually gifted and blessed beyond our perception of human greatness; unfortunately in recent years, his Christian integrity has been challenged, diverted, and trampled upon; without righteous discernment. Based on <u>ALL</u> of his Biblical Works of Art, Leonardo da Vinci indisputably understood that God's "curses and blessings" are **set-forth** before us within the universal Order of Time. Da Vinci's true Biblical legacy surpasses his physical existence of the Renaissance;

    *thus lived a man…*who visually documented on canvas the Bible sequences and milestones, and also painted depictions of heaven's mandates for salvation which is the core wisdom of Christianity;

    *thus lived a man…*who visually illustrated the divine "ORDER" of the **<u>Logos and Rhema</u>,** for the world to behold.

The Gift of the Palette

Da Vinci, artistically glorified and transfigured on canvas much of heaven's plan for eternal life. He ingeniously mastered the visual perspectives of God's Spiritual War; also the aspects of the Three Heavens, the Logos and Rhema…the Madonna of the Rocks, John the Baptist and the logic of the Lord's Last Supper.

Heretofore, the world has nearly lost Da Vinci's dynamics of the Feminine Physics of the Bible, the Four Hundred Years of Silence, and the Numeric Equations of the Lord God; the Godhead, and the cosmos. Leonardo da Vinci's spiritual paintings depict a wealth of profound messages and meanings from the Word of God.

This book reveals the rooted mysteries of Da Vinci's Renaissance and his layering techniques and methods of condensing Biblical events and wisdom throughout all of his spiritual works of art. This Biblical evidence of Da Vinci's holy compositions will exonerate the Artist's genuine Christian beliefs and loyalty to God. For nearly 500 years since Leonardo da Vinci's death, the elusive mysteries surrounding his gifted and blessed life are beginning to unfold; including his Christian values and his distaste of the earth's evils.

But, let it be known that in the end, the lone *sparrow* found a home amid a Royal Throne, leaving his magnificent gifts and heaven's **wisdom** for future generations.

The Biblical Truth of Da Vinci & God...Encoded
By: Miriam Parsons de Hostos

Heaven's mysteries revealed...

The Logos & The Rhema in the Da Vinci Renaissance

The Mystery Panels...the Metaphors of the Hebrew Reckoning of Day & Night - [Watches & Hours]

Heaven's Eviction @ 33.333333333 equation, Archangel Lucifer... 1/3 of Heaven's Angels

The Blood of Jesus could have **never** been contaminated in the earth's pool of genetics.

The X and Y Chromosomes of the Earth.

The Biblical Science of the Three Heavens

The Spiritual Paradox of "Time."

The "*Thought Physics*" of the earth's Geniuses; Savants

Miriam Parsons de Hostos
Creationism / Biblical Science,

www millgift.com.
gifts of the Holy Spirit

_____

The Glory of Creation
P. O. Box 1457
Bridgeport, Connecticut 06604

Table on Contents

Leonardo da Vinci,
the Master Artist of all Ages   Page 1

The Biblical Truth of
Leonardo da Vinci & God   Page 7

Da Vinci was a **Christian**…,
The Biblical Artist   Page 15

What's in a Name?
…….da Vinci?   Page 19

Leonardo da Vinci Sought
out Bible Wisdom   Page 24

Da Vinci…….and God's
Omnipresence   Page 29

The Attributes of God;
Ancient and Modern   Page 32

How Many **Heavens are Beheld**
in Da Vinci's Spiritual Art?   Page 42

The Biblical Feminine Physics…;
in Renaissance Paintings   Page 51

The Ancient **Predominance** of the
Masculine in the Christian Church Page 61

Table on Contents

The Homosexual Charges
of Da Vinci   Page 67

The Renaissance and the
Bible's Feminine Physics   Page 79

The Mystery of the Last Supper;
Crossroads of Law & Grace   Page 83

Decoding...,The Biblical Mystery of
         Da Vinci's Last Supper   Page 88

Decoding.......The Ancient **V** Symbol   Page 96

Decoding.......The Dualistic "**V**" Symbol   Page 99

Decoding.......The Roman Numeral 1000 (M)   Page 102

Decoding.......The Last Supper's Ceiling   Page 104

Decoding.......The Last Supper's Walls   Page 109

Decoding.......
The Mystery Panels...the Metaphors of the
Hebrew Reckoning of Day & Night
[Watches & Hours]   Page 113

Table on Contents

Decoding……..The Last Supper's Disciples	Page 118
Decoding……. The Last Supper's Windows	Page 124
Where is "The Last Supper's CHALICE?	Page 127
What is the Mystery of Mary Magdalene?	Page 130
The **X** Chromosome of Jesus	Page 144
The Biblical Blood & Lineage of Jesus	Page 163
Da Vinci's Wisdom of Shade and Light, thence, **Darkness**	Page 179
Whence, Cometh Gnostic…, Authority?	Page 183
Jesus and Mary Magdalene… A Holy Kiss or A Gnostic Kiss?	Page 185
The Biblical **Mystery**…. of the Madonna (s) of the Rocks	Page 193
Decoding……Version No. 1 The Madonna of the Rocks	Page 202

Table on Contents

Decoding.......Version No. 2
The Madonna of the Rocks   Page 234

The Biblical Mystery of
John the Baptist…Decoding   Page 244

The Biblical Mystery of the
Lady with an Ermine…
The Mistress & The Weasel   Page 250

The Biblical Mystery of the Three
Mary (s) at the Foot of the Cross   Page 265

Decoding…The Virgin Mary   Page 266

Decoding…Mary, the Aunt of Jesus   Page 268

Decoding…Mary of Magdala   Page 272

Leonardo Da Vinci's
Self Portrait   Page 276

What Did Da Vinci Know?   Page 281

Leonardo da Vinci
……..and God

Leonardo da Vinci, the Master Artist of All Ages.

Above all the Renaissance Artists, Leonardo da Vinci was the quintessential **GIFT** of the future.

The multiplicity of his exceptional talents and extraordinary artistic abilities enkindled the flames of knowledge and understanding to all the generations of the past five hundred years; hence, origin knowledge of the future.

During the past centuries, Da Vinci has been given the accolades of Genius, Visionary, Encoder, Brilliant, Charismatic, Servant of Kings, Man of all Season, and The Timeless Master Artist.

Nonetheless, it is seldom stated that it was **God** who blessed, protected, and gifted Leonardo da Vinci. God protected Leonardo throughout the silent rejection in his childhood and through the disappointments and hardships during his Renaissance life.

Leonardo da Vinci
……and God

In his lifetime, Leonardo da Vinci, suffered many stages of the Renaissance Status Quo; the Renaissance "lower class" stigma of the **FAMILY**, the strong arm of the **CHURCH,** and the unrests of the **STATE**, the ruling powers.

As an innocent child, Leonardo, inherited the stigma of illegitimacy; the mark of disgrace. Furthermore, Leonardo's father permanently segregated his own <u>SEED</u> to the lowest rank in society. By not giving Leonardo the family name, the child's inheritance was stripped and dissolved…, hence a Bastard Curse. Despite any psychological trauma he may have had as a child, God blessed him and turned evil for good…; *Romans 2:28 …And we know that all things work together for good to them that love God, to them who are the called according to his purpose.*

From a young man to adulthood, Leonardo da Vinci lived, at times, in a societal environment of unrest within the veil of evil rulers, sinister governments, the legalistic powers of the church and the shifting axis of misfortune. Although the Renaissance Era stood and still stands for rebirth and renewal of life, his environment still had an extensive and consequential degree of danger.

Page 3
Leonardo da Vinci
…….and God

However, despite the sorrows of his childhood, God stood guard and blessed this young man with transcendental wisdom and knowledge for modern civilization. God gifted Da Vinci with the intellectual and creative skills for the future; ingenious plans and designs for mankind's environment and surroundings; he was also gifted with the ability to portray on canvas the **visual** documentation of Biblical events.

All Gifts are from God

God's gifts to Leonardo da Vinci further encompassed the intellect and understanding of universal physics, geometry, botany, geography, anatomy, cosmology, draftsman, inventor, mathematician, water physics, alchemist, engineer, architect, sculptor, painter, Biblical encoder, Biblical science, spiritual annalist, and creationist.

Da Vinci was gifted in the Art of dimensional perspectives of the visual **past**, visual **present**, and the visual **future**. Da Vinci portrayed on canvas much of God's wisdom as it relates to the earth's spiritual war and the plan of salvation from heaven.

Leonardo da Vinci
…….and God

Da Vinci was a **Christian,** he was spiritually gifted in perspectives of Biblical equations and he fully understood the foundation of the divine "<u>ORDER OF GOD</u>". All of his Spiritual Art compositions majestically illustrated God's requirements and preconditions for mankind's salvation.

In the Renaissance Era, all of the master artists had the complete understanding of God's Code of Order, Code of Spiritual Numbers, and God's Codes of the Three Heavens. They also absolutely comprehended the spiritual wisdom of the Four Cardinal Directions and The Four Winds of the earth. However, much of the wisdom was not referred to as codes. It is only now in our time, *modern civilization*, that these perceived enigmas and mysteries are referred to as CODES, CODED, ENCODED, OR DECODED; hence, for Leonardo da Vinci and the Renaissance Age, it was **common knowledge to denote**, or *convey to the mind,* the Biblical aspects and visual messages of God and also the spiritual properties thereof.

Leonard da Vinci
…….and God

Leonardo da Vinci definitely transfigured and condensed his spiritual works of Art with Biblical messages of the <u>Fallen Earth, Salvation, and Christianity</u>, never, heresy as Dan Brown's Novel "The Da Vinci Code" alleges.

As Leonardo da Vinci's Biblically encoded masterpieces reveal, he knew the "Order-of-God," and he thoroughly understood the nature and the interconnection of God and Science; he also keenly knew the <u>spiritual physics</u> of the physical universe and the cosmos. Throughout his artistic career, God blessed Da Vinci with the **<u>visual</u>** wisdom of the Bible, the origins of life; creation, and the wisdom of eternal life for humanity.

In the Mind….., the wonderment of science and the inquisitiveness of science enriches and enhances all of life on the earth, *<u>but</u>* the creator and conductor of science is God. Only God gives Biology and Nature its universal directives; hence, Da Vinci stayed in awe of the essence of creation. Many of Leonardo's spiritual compositions illuminate with the wisdom of God's universe.

Leonardo da Vinci
…….and God

The Mystique of God and Da Vinci

Leonardo…;

here was a **CHILD,** who Biblically was the result of fornication, but yet God gifted him beyond the cosmos.

Leonardo da Vinci…;

here was a **MAN,** whose dynamic, ingenious, and extraordinary spiritual compositions reveal the hidden wisdom of the core of Christianity…, Encoded.

Furthermore, as the pages of this book will reveal, Leonardo da Vinci was also a Spiritual Annalist; most of his masterpieces chronologically penetrate the mysteries of God's divine plan and unveils heaven's wisdom for the earth; all encoded Biblically.

Page 7
Leonardo da Vinci
…….and God

The Biblical Truth of Leonardo da Vinci & God

In Dan Brown's Novel, **"The Da Vinci Code,"** it is alleged and inferred that Leonardo da Vinci was a heretic, one whose doctrine is contrary to the church, or a dissenter, a misbeliever who hid secrets in his paintings for fear of religious reprisals.

<u>As the evidence in this book will reveal, nothing is further from the truth</u>:

Leonardo da Vinci was **<u>NOT</u>** a heretic; his beliefs were of God and the Bible, never heresy. Dan Brown alleges that Da Vinci painted secret heretical clues into some of his famous pieces of Art. The novel claims that Da Vinci's composite of the Last Supper was encoded with the hidden secrets of a marriage and a bloodline between Jesus and Mary Magdalene; a bloodline alleged to exist today in the descendants of French Royalty. The Biblical evidence will reveal that Da Vinci's spiritual compositions were not encoded to hide any heretical beliefs.

Page 8
Leonardo da Vinci
…….and God

As this Book will reveal, Da Vinci had an astounding, profound, and humble belief in the Bible and God's **"ORDER;"** Leonardo's painting reveal God's Spiritual "ORDER"; the "ORDER" of creationism, and the "ORDER" of the cosmos, all of which are paralleled in the fullness of time.

Da Vinci knew the ramifications of Heaven's Spiritual War, and the physics of Spiritual Numerics; hence numerical ordinances of **Heaven's Spiritual War.**

This Book will decode the evidence and reveal the Biblical truths and mysteries of Da Vinci's spiritual paintings. It will also reveal the Biblical messages, meanings, and visual projections of his spiritual compositions.

Da Vinci had extraordinary knowledge and wisdom of Biblical **Warfare**, also God's Plan for humanity, *(all of heaven's souls)* and the annals of Biblical events of which he encoded into his Art; all with the specifics of Biblical content and meanings. Da Vinci had solid integrity for the things of God.

Leonardo da Vinci
…….and God

This unique artistry of encoding Art was **common ground** during the Renaissance Era; this technique was part of the Renaissance artistic method of **condensing** Biblical Wisdom and the spiritual value of the subject matter or event. However, Leonardo da Vinci's talents and technique of giving an epitome of **Vital Bible Content** in his spiritual art, surpassed all others; his paintings were the most discerned and pronounced in Biblical accuracy, also the most renowned in all of Art history; a gift that transcended all other artists. In essence, Da Vinci honored God.

Due to the numerous falsehoods, fiction, fabrications, and deceptions, in Dan Brown's Novel **"The Da Vinci Code,"** it is of the utmost importance to reveal the spiritual facts and truths of the Biblical mystique of Leonardo de Vinci's composite of "The Last Supper." For centuries Da Vinci's "Last Supper" has sparked reverence, amazement, and intrigue, but now it is being scrutinized by many towards the calibration of *Doubt*.

Page 10
Leonardo da Vinci
…….and God

Now, Dan Brown alleges that Da Vinci encoded "The Last Supper" with secrets of a **sacred union** of Christ and Mary Magdalene, and he also contends that the Apostle John at the right of Jesus in the painting is that of Mary Magdalene. Dan Brown further alleges that Jesus and Magdalene gave birth to a royal bloodline, hence, giving Jesus living descendants.

First and foremost, Leonardo Da Vinci painted some of his spiritual compositions with the Aura of the Feminine Factor. For instance, a few of Da Vinci's holy works of art, were painted with an outward semblance of the feminine physics. Indeed, Da Vinci also painted the composites of John Baptist with the feminine overtone. In the Renaissance Era, Artists purposely incorporated feminine and girlish features to the younger masculine in their art.

Unbeknown to the world today, the Renaissance Era unequivocally knew the **Science of Eve** and the association of the Earth's Feminine Physics…;
Genesis 3:20…And Adam called his wife's name Eve; because she was the mother of all living.

Leonardo da Vinci
…….and God

Also, **The Feminine Physics** in Da Vinci's paintings have and relate directly to the structure of Biblical Warfare from the origin **CURSE** of Genesis 3:15; a curse which was spoken by God to the serpent.

Scripture References:

Genesis 3:15…kjv
And I will put enmity between thee and the woman, and between thy seed and her seed; it shall bruise thy head, and thou shalt bruise his heel.

Genesis 3:16…kjv
Unto the woman he said, I will greatly multiply thy sorrow and thy conceptions; in sorrow thou shalt bring forth children; and thy desire shall be to thy husband, and he shall rule over thee.

Genesis 3:20…kjv
And Adam called his wife's name Eve; because she was the mother of all living.

1st Corinthians 11:8,,,kjv
For the man is not of the woman, but the woman of the man.

Leonardo da Vinci
…….and God

As Da Vinci's Biblical masterpieces reveal in this book, he encoded God's Biblical "ORDER," salvation's mandate, the configurations of Heaven's Spiritual War, and he encoded the complex structure and calculations of **Good verses Evil,** all in the perspectives **before and after** the fall of man; *Adam and Eve's sins.*

His Biblical Art captures and depicts unparalleled Biblical visuals of spiritual understanding and wisdom. In some of his paintings he also depicts the rage of the soul and boundaries of gravity's prison. Da Vinci also was the **cosmologist** of all cosmologists, because his silent brilliance captured the apex of God **with** Science; as his Vitruvian Man "**squares the radius**."

In refute of Dan Brown's claims, Da Vinci was very much in harmony with his Biblical beliefs and creation, which was the core of his inquisitiveness and intuitiveness from childhood to adulthood. The encoded spiritual masterpieces in this book, stunningly disclose his awesome and amazing knowledge of **God's Laws and Ordinances,** and the dynamics of creation's properties; physics thereof.

Leonardo da Vinci
…….and God

His encoded meanings and messages were not contrary to the church but are a resounding unity of Biblical doctrine and the structure of God; all the messages artistically encompassed to reveal the "Will" of God.. Most of his composites also expound and interpret Biblical disciplines, order, and stages thereof.

To reiterate, Leonardo was not a HERETIC, he was very aware of the curses and blessings of God; especially the severe penalties and consequences of chastisement, chastening, diseases, and death fermented to mankind and <u>owed for sin.</u> Leonardo da Vinci's own notes revealed his dismay and hate for the destruction of which EVIL ferments in the process of bidding for mankind's mental agreement; CHOICE.

<u>Biblical Discernment:</u>
Hence, each and everything of **<u>SIN</u>** has a consequence. Also, each and everything of **<u>DOUBT</u>** has a consequence; because it is the of lack of Biblical faith; inherent Word of God.

Doubt, **<u>calibrates two thoughts</u>**; hence, it divides and loosens mankind's spiritual sensitivity and allows unbelief to incubate. When the LORD first **<u>knocks</u>** at our door, faith in him is the key.

Leonardo da Vinci
…….and God

Faith in the Scriptures:

The Word of God, the Bible, is about faith; faith that God is; faith that God was; and faith that God will always be.

The Renaissance Artists <u>honored</u> God and the <u>scriptures</u>; hence, giving mankind the visual of God's mandates.

<u>Scripture Reference:</u>
<u>Luke 13:25…kjv</u>
When once the master of the house is risen up, and hath shut to the door, and ye begin to stand without, and to knock at the door, saying, Lord, Lord, open unto us; and he shall answer and say unto you, I know you not whence ye are:

Leonardo da Vinci
……was a Christian

Da Vinci was a **Christian**…; The Biblical Artist

Messages: What did Da Vinci Encode, Biblically?

The Encoded Biblical Evidence in Da Vinci's Spiritual Art Compositions Will Reveal the Following:

- The Authority of Spiritual War
- The Authority of the Three Heavens
- The Junctures of Biblical Turning Points
- The **FEMININE** Physics of the Bible
- The Masculine Physics of the Bible
- The Depictions of Renaissance Art **Dress Code**
- The **Four Hundred** (400) Years of Silence
- The Codes of the **Logos** and the **Rhema**
- The Properties of Darkness; hence, Shade
- The Numeric of the Cosmos

Leonardo da Vinci
……..was a Christian

Continued…Messages:
What did Da Vinci Encode, Biblically?

    The Numeric of Salvation

    The Mandate of Heaven, God's Plan

    The Amplitude of Omnipresence

    The **Jewish** Physics of Time

    The Perpetual Curse of the Tongue

    The Spiritual Differentiation of Botany

    The Constant Semblance of the **Biblical Feminine**

    The Spiritual **Perspectives** of the Past, Present, and Future. Hence, condensed wisdom.

Leonardo da Vinci magnificently portrayed all the dynamic intricacies and hidden aspects of God and the Bible. He also portrayed the condensed wisdom of God's "Spiritual War" on the earth, Satan's spiritual realm of power, and the technique of **Encoding Visual Scriptures.**

Leonardo da Vinci
.......was a Christian

As his Biblical Art reveal, Da Vinci equated The Study of Man, The Study of the Universe & Earth, and the Study of Biblical Creation, all of which are one in the **same**. Leonardo Da Vinci knew that God was the center of everything.

Da Vinci had the intellectual depth and insight of God's Spoken "ORDER," as his Biblically encoded masterpieces reveal.

Da Vinci also had a heart that loved life, and a heart that distinguished the difference between good and evil. When one Evaluates all the evidence and knowledge of Leonardo's paintings, it will be known that he painted life and renewal, also **love**; he painted and sketched the essence of creation, the origin of a human soul, the things of God, and facets of human behavior and the weapons of war. He further illustrated and painted instructional and foundational matters of "intellect and reasoning," and the understanding of numerous intellectual factors; and wisdom thereof.

Leonardo da Vinci
……..was a Christian

The **vast symphony** of Renaissance Spiritual Art Composites, are all rooted in Christianity and with the essence of God's Creations, The Masculine and Feminine Equations on the earth, with Human Factors of discipline, culture, and reasoning. They also painted with the Bible's Cosmic "ORDER," Heaven's Spiritual War, God's Salvation Plan for Mankind and/or the properties and mysteries of Biblical spiritual origins; hence physics thereof.

Some of the Master Artists painted the quintessence and serene elements of nature, the properties of creation's splendor. Others depicted the horrors of the earth's demonic forces; Satan's destruction of heaven's **Code of Conduct**.

The Master Art of Bernini, Botticelli, Chardin, De Caravagio, Michelangelo, Monet, Raphael, Da Messina and more, were rooted in the Biblical factors of God. They all comprehended the positive or negative aspects of Biblical Warfare and Creation.

Da Vinci…;
Fate of Childhood

What's in a Name?
………da Vinci

"What's in a name? That which we call a rose……By any other word would smell as sweet,"

Shakespeare posed this question in the famous love story of **"*Romeo and Juliet*"**; the star-crossed lovers were Romeo Montague and Juliet Capulet.

Ironically and unfortunately, The Renaissance Era believed that it was spiritually safer to name an illegitimate offspring after a town or city than a surname linked to fornication and generational curses, because a town does not sin; only man sins. In Da Vinci's Renaissance Era, the birthplace given to replace the surname was believed to curtail or **displace** the Bastard Curse of fornication. In retrospect, by Leonardo da Vinci not having a surname, his family's inheritance, it somewhat shielded him from imminent and impending generational curses; consequences of the deeds of his family; an absolute. Hence, it is believed that Leonardo da Vinci never married, which would have stopped the Bastard Curse, because his bloodline did not procreate.

Da Vinci…;
Fate of childhood

God takes the accounts of how a family discards a SEED……; descendants. God is also a God of Contractual Order, order of signatures, documents, oaths, vows, stewardship, thence, God will renders the curses, disciplines, or death to the origin of the evil doer of the deed.

WHAT'S IN A NAME?
That which we call… "de Vinci"?

What's in a Name? That which we call a Rose?.....The botanical classification. Nature does not sin.

What's in a Name? That which we call a Animal?.....The kingdom's designated species. The Animal Kingdom does not and cannot sin.

What's in a Name? That which we call a Montague?........The <u>Surname Montague</u> is subject to blessings and curses by God's laws, via generational deeds; Biblically.

Da Vinci…,
Fate of Childhood

What's in a Name? That which we call a Capulet? Capulet?.....The Surname of Capulet is subject to blessings and curses by God laws; via generational deeds; Biblically.

What's in a Name? That which we call "<u>de Vinci</u>"?

"OF VINCI, ITALY"……. A town cannot be easily <u>CURSED</u>.

The town of Vinci did not have an <u>Umbilical Cord</u> of heritage; the umbilical cord of mankind's inheritance of good and/or evil. Leonardo da Vinci was named after a town in Italy; hence, a town, country, or nation cannot be cursed, unless it is governed by the authorities of Satan, or a false god, or gods. For example: The tiny nation of Haiti was once given up to Satan and Voodoo; but the Church of Jesus Christ conquered the nation back for Christ in the late 1950's.

Da Vinci…,
Fate of Childhood

*The town of <u>VINCI</u> was under the authority of **Biblical** roots and beliefs and solemn oaths.*

A city or town also cannot be easily cursed, unless an unknown and mysterious demonic war tear its foundation; or if the land is given up demonically to Satan by the authoritative body of the ruling government.

However, isolated lands or acreages can be cursed by God if the SURNAMES or proprietors have demonic alliances and evil forces within their generations; equations thereof.

A family name, surname, can be a blessing or a curse, but a town or city, etcetera, cannot be easily cursed.

Da Vinci…,
Fate of Childhood

Leonardo did not inherit a family name; he did not have the honor or dishonor of a father's name, inheritance, because he was illegitimate; yet God blessed him exceedingly.

Using the name of Vinci **alone**, was probably a "lame" way out for Leonardo's father to escape or minimize further Biblical consequences.

What's in a Name?

Mankind has wages for sin, but a **Name** of a city, town, or country does not bear the wages; the accounts of individual sins are accumulated daily in heaven, each soul bears his own account to the Lord..

Reference Scriptures:
Romans 6:23…For the wages of sin is death; but the gift of God is eternal life through Jesus Christ our Lord.

What's in a SURNAME?

*……The **SINS** of its generation; hence, blessings and curses.*

Leonardo da Vinci
……. and God

Leonardo da Vinci Sought Out Biblical Wisdom

As his spiritual masterpieces reveal, Da Vinci sought out the wisdom and "ORDER" of God. He also aspired to understand the components of creationism because through his spiritual paintings, he magnificently projected the components and factors of God's Spiritual War on the earth. Da Vinci was extremely wise in the inter-connections of all living things and their origins.

The evidence of his spiritual Art reveal that Da Vinci wanted the focus of his commissioned compositions to be scripturally condensed. Many historians have written that Da Vinci never finished many of his commissioned work, but the mystery is that Da Vinci was a perfectionist to the perspectives of the present, past, and future of the Biblical history in question. Da Vinci never approached a commission with a conglomerate of meaningless spiritual ideas; he undertook and approached these compositions with scriptural **BACKBONE**.

Leonardo da Vinci
……..and God

Leonardo da Vinci knew the Bible, he visually illustrated and documented on canvas, the true logistics of Biblical events.

Did Da Vinci Trust in the Wisdom of God & The Bible? Yes, Indeed.

Da Vinci trusted God and the scriptures of the Bible. His compositions explode with wisdom, knowledge and understanding of God's universal "ORDER".

As the Last Supper reveals, Da Vinci put on canvas much of God's wisdom as it relates to the Earth's spiritual war and the plan of salvation from heaven; he also comprehended the pre-existence of God's spoken word.

In his composition, it is evident that Da Vinci studied the Biblical struggles and the laws of the Old Testament and the redeeming blood and rebirth in the New Testament. Da Vinci also depicts the Biblical order of plant life, the order of animal life, the order and authority of the fowl, the order of the feminine and masculine, the properties of darkness much of which he structurally encoded in condensed perspectives in his Art.

Leonardo da Vinci
…….and God

Biblical Discernment:
Does the <u>World</u> Today Trust God & The Bible? The Answer is NO.

Much of the world today trusts and embraces the Bible <u>ONLY</u> for it's medicinal and nutritional values; the world today, trusts and refers to the Bible for military tactics, maneuvers, and secrets of wars and battles. The world also trusts the Bible for the intellect of cosmology, astronomy, hence, they search the Bible for knowledge of archaeology, oceanography, and anthropology, and mapping the earth; the world further searches the Bible for lost cities, lost treasure, and as an ancient compass.

Hence, the Bible is a composite of the beginning of time, God's Word, Love, Laws, commandments, spiritual war, procurement of land, spiritual redemption, sacrifices, historical covenants, doctrine, love letters, and end times.

Leonardo da Vinci
…….and God

In summary, most of the **World** does not trust God & the Bible, the *Apostate* **Church,** does not trust God and the infallible Bible; **Governments** do not trust God and the Holy Bible.

Matthew 6:33…kjv:
But seek ye first the kingdom of God, and his righteousness; and all these things shall be added unto you.

<u>Luke 12:31…kjv</u>
But rather seek ye the kingdom of God; and all these things shall be added unto you.

Hollywood also trusts the Bible for theater and drama. Governments, trusts the Bible for the structure of law and order, governments also trust the Bible for their **irrevocable OATHS;** mankind further utilizes the Bible for psychic factors;

Leonardo da Vinci
……..and God

HENCE…, much of humanity trusts the Bible for many, many aspects of life's mysterious, intellectual value, and intrigue…… BUT for the **SALVATION of the SOUL,** the Bible is most often **REJECTED.**

The Bible is NOT a Research Book; the Bible is the WORD and WISDOM of God for believers "IN CHRIST." The Bible is God's doctrine for mankind's Salvation in conjunction with the Holy Spirit. The Bible has the Laws, commandments, and Order for the **AGENT OF "Free- Will";** mankind.

WISDOM: Scripture Reference
Job 38:36-37…kjv
Who hath put wisdom in the inward parts? Or who hath given understanding to the heart? 37 Who can number the clouds in wisdom? Or who can stay the bottles of heaven,

Da Vinci.......
and God's Omnipresence

Leonardo da Vinci and some of the Renaissance master artists painted with a unique Spiritual Technique of which captured the aura of God's omnipresence.

Most of the Renaissance Christians knew that the universe has only **ONE TRUTH**; the truth of the Biblical God and the dominance of his omnipresence and of his omniscience. When the spirit of God in *Genesis 1:2*, moved upon the face of the waters, it never left the earth…; creationism continued it's spiritual directives.

In Biblical reality the physics of **nothing** and the physics of **something** possesses a perpetual constant of the omnipresence of God upon the earth; Genesis 1:2.

Genesis 1:2…kjv

And the earth was without form, and void; and darkness was upon the face of the deep. And the Spirit of God moved upon the face of the waters.

Da Vinci …and God's Omnipresence

In some of his masterpieces, Da Vinci ingeniously articulates creationism with the **accompaniment** of science.

Most of the Renaissance Artists knew God's Journey of *time* which <u>encompasses</u> all of creation, the war of heaven, salvation for mankind; ***agents of free-will***, heaven on earth, justice and law, and the demise of Satan….. all **girded and embodied** in the omnipresence of God. Angels also stand in the presence of God's physics; Luke 1:19.

The Renaissance Era did not circumvent or side-step GOD, they knew the dominant forces of the omnipresence of God and the cosmos. Of course, they probed in science and all the intricate facets of the intellect thereof, but their inquisitiveness of science never replaced the essence of God.

Of course, the Renaissance Era also had its share of ruthless evildoers, cut throat rulers, sinister plots, legalistic mandates and crimes of the church, and the perpetual dime of greed and power. But, nevertheless, the innocent factions of the Renaissance Era maintained the essence of rebirth. The gifts of the Master Artists rendered the Biblical <u>visuals</u> of the things of God's and his eternal love for man.

Da Vinci...
and God's Omnipresence

Yes indeed, Da Vinci also studied the wonders of science. Science is the systematic study of the universe and the physical world; hence, science encompasses all of God's breath of life and the stealth powers that dwell within his ordinances, laws, and commandments, all of which are inlaid in the structured design of the earth and cosmos.

All Sciences function in an inherent interrelated and interconnected composition of divine "**ORDER**". All the sciences are structured and maneuvered by divine ordinances; science is obeys the commands of God; their components and genetics processes will not exert **without** the allowances or disallowances of God and his omnipresence.

Leonardo da Vinci had a profound respect, honor, and love for the silence of God's presence; the internal fabric of his sovereign rule.

The Attributes of God; <u>Ancient</u> & Modern

The Ancient Knew the Attributes of God, and his wrath.

The Renaissance Knew…,The Ancient of Days…….; God.

<u>Daniel 7:9…kjv</u>
I beheld till the thrones were cast down, and the Ancient of days did sit, whose garment was white as snow, and the hair of his head like the pure wool: his throne was like the fiery flame, and his wheels as burning fire.

God's attributes are infinite; he is the vast eternal breath of life. The Renaissance Artists knew the attributes and mysteries of God; they studied and depicted God's goodness, wrath, heaven's directives and the culprit of the mind. They also studied the "Four Hundred Years of Silence" when God, <u>barred</u> all further wisdom and knowledge from his people; at the end of the Book of Malachi.

The Attributes of God;
Ancient & Modern

God's Attributes

*The attributes are adhered to the **DIVINE ORDER**, **LAWS**, and RIGHTEOUSNESS of God:*

God is Holy

God is infinite

God is masculine

God is omniscient

God is our creator

God does grieve

God is logarithmic

God logs deferred labor; logos

God is the creator of all things

God is the owner of all souls

God knows and sees the future

God never sleeps or slumbers

God is complete perfection

God is a severe conservative

God is not an author of confusion

God is not religious

God's spiritual war has finite mathematics

God's Spirit has infinite mathematics

God's Heaven has three Jerusalem (s)

God's Word is infallible: The Holy Bible

God is Sovereign

God is omnipresent

God is omnipotent

God is our father

God does not pain

God is 1/3 geometric

God is mathematics

The Attributes of God; Ancient & Modern

*The attributes are adhered to the DIVINE ORDER, <u>**LAWS**</u>, and RIGHTEOUSNESS of God:*

God is a God of Stewardship

God is three dimensional

God has only one provision for salvation

God knows all lineages from the origin of Adam

God does not answer all prayers

God's ruby is a moral family

God is a God of origin

God <u>orchestrates</u> all of <u>Science</u>

God is a God of seven spiritual components

God communicates with all of nature; daily

God is a God of code, order, ordinances

God is the elegant design of the universe

God orders the steps of the righteous

God knows the Love of your life

God breaths in the glow of innocence

God is not a respecter of persons

God is a God of authoritative dress code

God rides the wind and storms

God has ten commandments, not suggestions

God is the same today, yesterday and tomorrow

God is a stealth disciplinarian

The Attributes of God; Ancient and Modern

*The attributes are adhered to the DIVINE ORDER, **LAWS**, and RIGHTEOUSNESS of God:*

God is a God of moral alphabet

God is complete love, fused with stationary laws

God uses war for chastening and castigating

God composes war, owed, for sin

God allows wars, per our choice to sin

God releases knowledge in measured time

God is a 99.9% surveyor of his money

God's angels attack sin to protect God

God hears all speech from the <u>TONGUE</u>, daily

God's Spirit requires faith in his son Jesus

God punishes or destroys all pastors that destroy and scatter the sheep of his pasture

God allows our mind to believe the deceit of our heart

God will destroy nations who <u>legislate</u> immorality

God's Spirit will thrust immoral governments in derision

God will impose on the meek, to shift governments

God also composes floods, earthquakes, famine, fires, plagues, and diseases

The Attributes of God;
Ancient and Modern

God's Spirit will rebuke religions' conjoined agreements

God's Spirit rebukes any division of Jesus and the Sword

Malachi 3:6…
For I am the LORD, I change not;

Isaiah 55:8…
For my thoughts are not your thoughts, neither are your ways my ways, saith the LORD

Biblical Discernment:

……Hence, even the **PAGAN** MARINERS with Jonah, knew the God of the Bible

Pagans with Jonah

Scripture Reference:

<u>*Jonah 1:5…..kjv*</u>

Then the mariners were afraid, and cried every man unto his god, and cast forth the wares that were in the ship into the sea, **to** *lighten it of them. But Jonah was gone down into the sides of the ship; and he lay, and was fast asleep.*

The Attributes of God; Ancient and Modern

Jonah 1:6.....kjv
So the shipmaster came to him, and said unto him, What meanest thou, O sleeper? Arise, call upon thy God, if so be that God will think upon us, that we perish not.

Jonah 1:14.....kjv
Wherefore they cried unto the LORD, and said, We beseech thee, O LORD, we beseech thee, let us not perish for this man's Life, and lay not upon us innocent blood: for thou, O LORD, has done as it pleased thee.

When mankind repents at 180 degrees, he dwells within the teachings, laws, and commandments of the Lord; grace. In Biblical repentance one turns away from sin……..; BUT, if mankind repents at 360 degrees he has deceived himself and gives way to the weaver's shuttle, curses and severe punishments because God is HOLY and his son taught three years (3) of conduct and behavior <u>BEFORE</u> he purchased us back from sin, which released all of humanity from underneath "<u>Spiritual Marshall Law</u>."

*Furthermore, when the Word of God is not obeyed, God allows the spirit of error, the author of confusion to enter "**<u>thought</u>;**" the mind of man, thence, spiritual warfare.*

The Attributes of God; Ancient and Modern

ALL WISDOM COMES FROM GOD

After The Middle Ages, with all its destruction, it was God's Spirit that worked it's way through the **Corridors of the Human "Mind"** via the Age of the Renaissance. The Fourteenth Century was the rediscovery of the wisdom, knowledge, understanding, rebirth and renewal.

Scripture Reference:
All intellect comes from God:
Isaiah 11:2…kjv
And the spirit of the LORD shall rest upon him, the spirit of wisdom and understanding, the spirit of counsel and might, the spirit of knowledge and of the fear of the LORD;

Jeremiah 4:22, 23…kjv

For my people is foolish, they have not known me; they are sottish children, and they have none understanding; They are wise to do evil, but to do good they have no knowledge. 23 I beheld the earth, and, lo, it was without form, and void; and the heavens, and they had no light.

The Attributes of God; Ancient and Modern

Da Vinci knew the ramifications of sin; he himself was marked by the stigma of fornication and he was psychologically demoted for the rest of his life because of the origin of his birth in the Renaissance Era; hence, God turned all for good

Most of God's attributes measure and weigh the accounts of sin.

*God is a God of Order, Ordinances, Mercy Love **with** Laws, Commandments and Stewardship.*

The Attributes of God;
Ancient and Modern

The Spiritual War perpetuates daily; God allows sin to be judged daily. Humanity; lives in a fallen earth, hence, <u>God's Spiritual Warfare is twenty-four hours per day</u>, everyday. The Christians "In Christ" must carry the cross daily with the grace and mercy of Jesus.

<u>Matthew 16:24-27…kjv</u>
Then said Jesus unto his disciples, If any man will come after me, let him deny himself, and take up his cross, and follow me. 25 For whosoever will save his life shall lose it: and whosoever will lose his life for my sake shall find it. 26 For what is man profited, if he shall gain the whole world, and lose his own soul? Or what shall a man give in exchange for his soul? 27 For the Son of man shall come in the glory of his Father with his angels; and then he shall reward everyman according to his works.

<u>Ephesians 6:11-12</u>
Put on the whole armour of God, that ye may be able to stand against the wiles of the devil. 12 For we wrestle not against flesh and blood, but against principalities, against powers, against the rulers of the darkness of this world, against spiritual wickedness in high places.

The Attributes of God;
Ancient and Modern

2nd Corinthians 6:1-2

We then, as workers together with him, beseech you also that ye receive not the grace of God in vain. 2(For he saith, I have heard thee in a time accepted, and in the day of salvation have I succoured thee: behold, now is the accepted time; behold, now is the day of salvation.)

The attributes of God are profoundly innumerable, but Leonardo da Vinci had a genuine understanding of the mysteries, characteristics, and the wisdom of God as the evidence of his ART penetrates the human soul.

Leonardo da Vinci…
and the Three Heavens

How Many <u>Heavens are Beheld</u> in Da Vinci's Spiritual Art?

Da Vinci and most of the Renaissance Artist painted the realms of the Three Heavens, Biblically. They knew and depicted the radius of heavenly boundaries. In the Sistine Chapel in Rome, Michael Angelo depicts the greatest visual interpretations of heavens dimensions and balanced proportions.

We must remember that the EARTH is the dominant part of the cosmos. The Archangel Lucifer, was cut to the ground by God for pride and arrogance; the war of heaven was ignited when Lucifer deemed to exalt himself above God. Lucifer, the prideful and arrogant **creation** asserting himself against his sovereign **CREATOR**; hence, God struck him down to the earth.

Isaiah 14.12 How art thou fallen from heaven, O Lucifer, son of the morning! how art thou cut down to the ground, which didst weaken the nations!

Leonardo da Vinci…
and the Three Heavens

The earth is 1/3 (one third) part of heaven. Lucifer and his fallen angel consists of the 1/3 the percentage of the origin of heaven's realm.

When Lucifer was cut to the earth, the numeric of the universe was catastrophically altered; hence, the Renaissance Era had a complete and thorough understanding of the physics of heaven's symmetry.

Leonardo da Vinci also painted the realms of spiritual authorities of the three heavens throughout his spiritual compositions. He had superb knowledge of heaven's spacial dimensions of the first, second, and third heaven.

God is omnipresent in the third heaven, God is omnipresent in the second heaven, and omnipresent in the first heaven. The third heaven is the Command Headquarters of God and his angels; the second and first heaven is the Spiritual Battle Field for God's souls; the spiritual battle with the principalities of darkness; the battle for the **MIND OF MAN.**

Leonardo da Vinci
…and the Three Heavens

*The following are some of the paintings that encompass and identify the realms of the **Three Heavens**:*

1- The Last Supper
   Depicts the wisdom of the 1st and 2nd Heaven

2- The Madonna of the Rocks 1483
   This depiction encompasses the 3rd Heaven

3- The Madonna of the Rocks 1490
   This depiction encompasses of the 1st Heaven.

4- <u>PRELUDE, The Old Testament:</u>
   *Madonna and Child with a **<u>Pomegranate</u>**, ca. 1470*
   *This depiction is the 1st Heaven **<u>before sin</u>**.*

5- <u>MANIFESTATION, The New Testament:</u>
   *Madonna and Child with the **<u>Carnation</u>**, ca.1473*
   *This composite depicts the 1st Heaven **<u>after sin</u>**.*

Leonardo da Vinci
…and the Three Heavens

The Three Heavens are also known as the Three Jerusalem (s).

Many have asked……Where is heaven and what is heaven?

Mankind lives in the fallen heaven. **One-Third** of heaven was struck down to the earth; The EARTH is a vital part of heaven.

Lucifer, cut to the ground; Iniquity was found in him, *Ezekiel 28:15……Thou was perfect in they ways from the day that thou wast created, till iniquity was found in thee.*

The Biblical numeric of **Lucifer** and his fallen angels on earth is 33.3333333 (33%).

The Biblical Numeric of our savior **Jesus** for the Fallen Earth is 33.3333333 (33%).

Leonardo da Vinci
….and the Three Heavens

The **Mathematical** Equations of the Three Heavens:

The **Authoritative Powers** of the Universe; Hence, Laws of physics, Biblically:

<u>The Inverted Triangle; laws and ordinances</u>
Totals……………..99.999999999 Infinite
3rd Heaven   33.333333333
2nd Heaven   33.333333333
1st Heaven   33.333333333

Matthew 28:18……..And Jesus came and spake unto them, saying, All power is given unto me in <u>heaven</u> and in <u>earth</u>.

The Authoritative Powers of the Earth; the Fallen Heaven…; hence, laws of physics, Biblically:

<u>The Triangle; laws and commandments</u>
1st Heaven   33.3333333
2nd Heaven   33.3333333
3rd Heaven   33.3333333
Totals……………….99.9999999 Finite

Leonardo da Vinci
…and the Three Heavens

Infinite became finite and ascended back to infinity.

*Our Lord Savior, **Thirty-three** plus infinity*

*We are particles and substances of the universe; divinely connected to the Origin of "**Order**;" perfection.*

Reference Scripture:
2nd Corinthians 12:1-3…kjv
It is not expedient for me doubtless to glory. I will come to visions and revelations of the Lord. 2 I knew a man in Christ above fourteen years ago, (whether in the body, I cannot tell; or whether out of the body, I cannot tell: God knoweth;) such an one caught up to the third heaven. 3 And I knew such a man, (whether in the body, or out of the body, I cannot ell: God knoweth;) 4 How that he was caught up into paradise, and heard unspeakable words, which it is not lawful for a man to utter.

Leonardo da Vinci
...and the Three Heavens

Heaven's Archangels **Before Lucifer's** Iniquity:

*In the beginning, this was the origin "ORDER" of creation science of the heavens; the celestial and terrestrial **glory** of the cosmos.*

Archangel Gabriel:
*$1/3^{rd}$ of the **Third** heaven........33.333333333*

Archangel Michael:
*$1/3^{rd}$ of the **Second** Heaven.....33.333333333*

Archangel Lucifer:
*$1/3^{rd}$ of the **First** Heaven........33.333333333*

Total Host of Hosts..................99.999999999

Leonardo da Vinci
…and the Three Heavens

The Archangels **Lucifer, After Iniquity**:

WAR IN HEAVEN

The mathematical equation of Lucifer;
Old Testament:
Lucifer…… **66.666666666**
Cut to the ground 1st and 2nd Heaven

> *Isaiah 14:12…How art thou fallen from heaven, O Lucifer, son of the morning! How art thou cut down to the ground, which didst weaken the nations!*

> *Revelation 12:7,8,9….And there was war in heaven: Michael and his angels fought against the dragon; and the dragon fought and his angels, And prevailed not: neither was their place found any more in heaven. And the great dragon was cast out, that old serpent, called the Devil, and Satan, which* **<u>deceiveth the whole world</u>**: *he was cast out into the earth, and his angels were cast out with him.*

> *Luke 10:18…And he said unto them, I beheld Satan as lightning fall from heaven.*

Leonardo da Vinci
...and the Three Heavens

The Ancient Evidence of the Three Heavens in the Modern Day:

The most vivid evidence of the THREE (3) HEAVENS in today's modern society can be seen in the ornate churches of the Russian and Greek Orthodox crucifixes. These Christian Orthodox steeple crucifixes show and reveal the THREE dimensions of heaven. Their ornate crucifixes have **Three Cross Bars** within the one Vertical Beam of the structure.

The first (1st) **TOP CROSS BAR** represents the Third Heaven (3rd heaven).

The second (2nd) **MIDDLE CROSS BAR** represents the Second Heaven (2nd heaven).

The third (3rd) **BOTTOM BAR is CROSSED at a SLANT,** referring to the cursed dimension that of earth; the fallen earth.

The third **BOTTOM BAR** of the Orthodox Crucifix represents the logistics of the status of the earth, indicative of the fallen man with the downward slant of the BAR of the CROSS.

Da Vinci's Art…and
the Biblical Feminine Physics

The Biblical <u>Feminine</u> Physics…, in Renaissance Paintings.

The Renaissance Christians understood and recognized the existence of the <u>Feminine Physics</u>; hence, mystery thereof.

Da Vinci painted specific spiritual masterpieces with the <u>auras</u> of the Earth's Fallen Feminine; Physics thereof.

<u>*Scripture References:*</u>
Genesis 3:15…And I will put enmity between thee and the woman, and between they seed and her seed; it shall bruise thy head, and thou shalt bruise his heel.

Genesis 3:20…And Adam called his wife's name Eve; because she was the mother of all living.

Leonardo de Vinci's Era comprehended the mystery of the <u>Biblical Feminine Physics</u> and the <u>Masculine "ORDER" of Heaven</u> and how they inter-related in the fallen earth.

Da Vinci's Art…and
the Biblical Feminine Physics

Adam, the Man of Creation was formed of the dust of the ground; and woman from man.

Genesis 2:7…
And the LORD formed man of the dust of the ground, and breathed into his nostrils the breath of life; and man became a living soul.

1- *The Man was created by God of the dust of the ground.*
2- *The Man was created in the radiances of the daylight.*
3- *The Woman is made of the Man; genetics of Masculine.*
4- *The Woman was made in the physics of the evening;*

Genesis 2:22…
And the rib, which the LORD God had taken from man, made he a woman, and brought her unto the man.

The physics of the Feminine was created from the "Masculine Order" of God. Biblically, the genetics of the feminine is of the masculine bone substance; the RIB is the bone and marrow that **is** the flesh of Adam's flesh; the DNA of the genetics **curve**.

Page 53
Da Vinci's Art…and
the Biblical Feminine Physics

Eve's genetics was of the marrow, the curve, (DNA) from the masculine genetics of the man who was **ALREADY PRE-CREATED**. Adam, was Eve's direct authority. Adam was ready **pigmented** with all the chromosomes of creation, made in the image and likeness of God.

Before the origin of SIN, the masculine and feminine were of one creation; one creation of one authority. God was Adam's authority… and Adam was Eve's spiritual and structured authority.

In the Garden of Eden, the feminine was the first to be deceived. Sin came into the world **by way** of the feminine choice; the female's free-will.

The physics of the "Feminine" was sexually seduced by the serpent; she was spiritually seduced in "*thought*" and in the flesh. Before the fall of *the masculine*, Eve was the first to fall in complete agreement with the serpent. The **Feminine**, Eve, was the first to disobey God; she was enthralled with evil. Hence, she was the first to encounter an internal state of spiritual segregation from Adam and God; Eve was the first to encounter the fruit of the serpent, the knowledge of Evil.

Da Vinci's Art…and the Biblical Feminine Physics

Eve was thrust under the subjection of Satan; the feminine physics was now under the status of evil's subjection, which caused, thereafter, the **MASCULINE** of God to fall also in disobedience.

Now, who deceived Adam?……It was Eve, in conjunction with the spiritual authority of which she gave to Satan.

The Science of the Fallen Eve is the root of the Feminine Physics of which God had spoken the PERMANENT GENETIC CURSES of Genesis 3:15 and Genesis 3:16, that of which all exist today. Leonardo da Vinci painted many of these aspects and detailed visuals of the FALLEN FEMININE of the earth.

Genesis 3:15…And I will put enmity between thee and the woman, and between they seed and her seed; it shall bruise thy head, and thou shalt bruise his heel.

Genesis 3:16…Onto the woman he said, I will greatly multiply thy sorrow and they conception; in sorrow thou shalt bring forth children; and thy desire shall be to thy husband, and he shall rule over thee.

Da Vinci's Art…and the Biblical Feminine Physics

In Dan Brown's Novel "The Da Vinci Code" the essence and mystery of the Sacred Feminine is the core of his theory; of a bloodline of Jesus and Mary Magdalene. The Renaissance captured on canvas the Biblical feminine as it related to the <u>FALLEN EVE</u>, the factors of the **Feminine Under-the-Law**, and the factors of the **Feminine "In-Christ."**

All these Feminine Factors were incorporated into all of Leonardo da Vinci's Spiritual Arts. One of the mysteries of the Biblical Feminine and the Renaissance Master Artists was that they illustrated the feminine status in conjunction with feminine virtue or offenses against God. These Master Artists, conveyed to the <u>visual mind</u> on canvas the virtuous feminine, and they also tastefully illustrated the accumulative demonic forces of the Feminine Spiritual Physics as it related to her sins and sexual liaisons. ***There Is Nothing New Under the Sun***……The Renaissance firmly understood the demonic factors of multiple sexual bonds of the feminine that dwell "**Out-of-Christ**."

Stemming back from the Medieval Era, the **masculine** was very aware of the curses of sexual bonds; they **becometh one flesh**. In many sinister plots, the FEMININE would meet an early demise or a "so-called" untimely death brought on by the **masculine's** determination to avoid the demonic curses from illicit affairs.

Da Vinci's Art…and
the Biblical Feminine Physics

Nonetheless, Mary Magdalene was never the sacred feminine of a divine marriage; she was simply a humble servant of the Lord who was saved during the crossroads of The Law and Crucifixion. For Mary Magdalene to have become the Sacred Feminine in marriage and also starting a bloodline with Jesus, the act of this marital union would have fatally **cancelled** the entire salvation plans of God for all of mankind on the earth.

The Serpent - Reference Scriptures:
Genesis 3:1…kjv
Now the serpent was more subtle than any beast of the field which the LORD God had made. And he said unto the woman, Yea, hath God said, Ye shall not eat of every tree of the garden?

Genesis 3:4 - 5…kjv
And the serpent said unto the woman, Ye shall Not surely die: 5 For God doth know that in the day ye eat thereof, then your eyes shall be opened, and ye shall be as gods, knowing good and evil.

Much of Ancient civilizations and the Renaissance Artists absolutely knew the Science of Eve, but in recent centuries the wisdom and evidence has been lost or applied to fables, myths, and fairy tales. Yet, in recent times the subtle power struggles of the masculine and feminine escapes the psychoanalysts. The psychoanalyst Sigmund Freud once asked himself, a baffling question of the feminine…**"What does a WOMAN want?"**

Da Vinci's Art…and the Biblical Feminine Physics

Sigmund Freud asked……, "What does a Woman want?" Hence, she wants what her Biblical and Creation origins did **not** genetically grant her, that of the divine factors of the earth's **Primary Spiritual Authority** and the **Logos Physiology;** these are sequences of nature, all of which were given unto the **masculine by God**; heaven's pre-ordained authorities.

Of course, the Feminine Physics, is not a source for modern day discrimination; the mystery is inherent in creation science and the medical sciences; she is from the origin of the masculine.

<<<+>>>

The Biblical Feminine Factors…"for the man is not of the woman; but the woman of the man.

Of course, in the New Testament the feminine and the masculine are both equal; this is the unity of genuine repentance and saved souls when they confess to the Lord and live **"IN-CHRIST" JESUS**.

Da Vinci's Art…and
the Biblical Feminine Physics

The Feminine Physics
A Biblical and Creation <u>Absolute</u>

1st Timothy 2:11,12,13,…kjv
Let the woman learn in silence with all subjection. 12 But I suffer not a woman to teach, nor to usurp authority over the man, but to be in silence. 13 For Adam was first formed, then Eve.

<u>The Feminine Physics was deceived, not Adam.</u>

1st Timothy 2:14…kjv
And Adam was not deceived, but the woman being deceived was in the transgression.

In most of today's modern society, the notion that "*the woman was made of the man*" is all but a fairy tale in the veils of societal unbelief. Eighty percent (80%) of society today does not belief the Bible in its totality as the inherent Word of God; many believe that Adam and Eve is a mere fairy tale of Christianity, and that only **<u>Evolution</u>** is the King of Jungle.

Da Vinci's Art…and
the Biblical Feminine Physics

The <u>Gender</u> of the Christ could <u>not</u> have been…Feminine

Biblically, God could not have sent a Feminine Savior…, because God himself is of "Masculine Authority and **Order**."

In the beginning, the masculine "ORDER" was Adam. After the fall of man, the "ORDER OF GENDER" of the Savior to come, for the redemption of mankind… was of the divine mandate of the masculine fabric of God.

Isaiah 54:5…..kjv
For they Maker is thine husband;_ the LORD of hosts is his name; and they Redeemer the Holy One of Israel; The God of the whole earth shall he be called.

The "ORDER" of the **Third Heaven is Masculine**

The "ORDER" of the Second Heaven and First Heaven dwell in the Spiritual War with Satan, who is the prince and power of the air. These two heavens have the numerical equations of sixty-six. **Before Sin**, the feminine was made of the masculine "<u>order</u>" in the First Heaven and the **Gender of Christ** was ordered from the masculine "<u>ORDER</u>" of God in the Third Heaven.

Da Vinci's Art…and the Biblical Feminine Physics

Reference Scriptures

Ephesians 2:2

Wherein in time past ye walked according to the course of this world, according to the prince of the power of the air, the spirit that now worketh in the children of disobedience:

Ephesians 6:12

For we wrestle not against flesh and blood, but against principalities, against powers, against the rulers of the darkness of this world, against spiritual wickedness in high places.

The Feminine origin is of **ONE** flesh, from the genetics of the masculine. Sin, and the cursed earth of Genesis 3:17 separated their genetics and spiritual physics. The Feminine was created of masculine biology and DNA; masculine origin.

Cursed Ground
Scripture Reference:

Genesis: 3:17…KJV

And unto Adam he said, Because thou hast hearkened unto the voice of thy wife, and hast eaten of the tree, of which I commanded thee, saying, Thou shalt not eat of it cursed is the ground for thy sake; in sorrow shalt thou eat of it all the days of thy life;

Page 61
Da Vinci's Art...and
the Biblical Feminine Physics

The Ancient <u>Predominance</u> of the Masculine in the Christian Church

*The Renaissance Master Artist and the Christian ancestors, understood the spiritual predominance of the <u>**MASCULINE**</u> in the Christian Church.*

In modern times the struggles of woman in the church hierarchy has come under much debate and rejection in some denominations, especially the role of women in the Roman Catholic Church.

What is the enigma of the masculine superiority in the Christian Church hierarchy? This enigma has a twofold truth that the **secular** world and the **science** world reject. First and foremost, the reason relates to the irrefutable "MASCULINE ORDER" of God that renders the ancient dominance of authority; God is masculine, the Lord is masculine, the Holy Spirit is masculine, and Adam was created masculine.

Da Vinci's Art…and
the Biblical Feminine Physics

The second truth of origin relates to the deception and downfall of the "Feminine Help Meet" of Genesis 2:18. Eve, the feminine, was the first to adapt and calibrate the **knowledge of evil** into human "*thought*." Hence, the feminine mind was the first to fall in conjoined agreement with the spiritual content of evil, the realm of the serpent. Furthermore, the ancient, associated the woman to be vulnerable with Satan because the Messiah was going to be birthed by a woman; the feminine factor. A **WOMAN** was going to birth the Messiah, hence, Satan prepared to attack the essence of woman. What woman? Satan did not know; but the "ancient" knew that Satan was after the woman and, of course, it is perceived that she is the easier to be tempted. This has been a **feminine stigma** since the beginning of sin; Eve and Satan's conjoined agreement of origin; hence, disobedience against God.

In the garden……, it was the woman's transgression that forced the collapse of procreation within the explicit righteousness of God's realm; **divine righteousness with righteousness**. It was the woman's transgression that forced the **fruits of conception** of Adam and Eve *into* the realm and authority of good and evil.

Da Vinci's Art…and the Biblical Feminine Physics

1st Timothy 2:14…kjv
And Adam was not deceived, but the woman being deceived was in the transgression.

The root of the mystery also dwells in the factors of Satan and in the spiritual authorities of the Church's anointed powers to **cast out demons**. Spiritually, the casting out of demons, or casting out of evil spirits, or the rituals of an exorcism in ancient times, was 90% spiritually successful with the **dominance of the masculine authority,** because Satan sought out the feminine factors and Satan was and is an expert on SCRIPTURES.

The Feminine Factors must be in the correct spiritual status with the scriptures. Biblically, the Masculine **"Order"** is never under the spiritual subjection of the feminine; even under-grace, God gives the **masculine… first authority**.

Hence, Satan could and would immediately protest an exorcism from the feminine factors. Satan is the accuser, Satan will challenge God on his own righteousness.

Da Vinci's Art…and the Biblical Feminine Physics

Satan could and would question God about the feminine status as follows: Is she "in-Christ"? Is she under the **subjection of a husband** "in-Christ," or is she her husband's authority? Is she a maiden under the authority of a father that dwells "in-Christ"? Is she a divorced clergy within the <u>five-fold ministries</u> of Ephesians 4:11, "In-Christ"? Is she a Gay clergy? Is she pro-life? Does she rewrite or reject portions of the Bible? Is she living in a fornication status? ……In the realm of casting out demons, Satan has more leverage against the feminine status. Satan is **PROFICIENT** in scripture and Lord of the Flies.

God is Masculine and the Third Heaven is of the Masculine Order. For centuries, especially in the Old Testament, the casting out of demons or exorcism was kept in the realm of the **MASCULINE ORDER**.

The Biblical account is that the woman was the first to be deceived by Satan and the first to **accommodate the mind** (Brain) with the knowledge of Evil. Eve was the first to receive the **BATON** of evil knowledge. Her "<u>thoughts</u>" were the first to receive the influx of the **right brain's** hemispheric characteristics; hence, Adam was not deceived, but the woman being deceived was in the transgression.

Da Vinci's Art…and
the Biblical Feminine Physics

In the 21st Century……, the Feminine Clergy Perception:

Where Have All God's Flowers Gone?

Unlike ancient times, in these modern times it's perceived and in some cases extremely transparent that some liberal factions of the feminine clergy exude the residue of the masculine demeanor within the limelight of pride and stealth arrogance. In most cases she is a **deceived** force with votes and stature; lobbying in the **world's** corridors with an urgent desire to break heaven's glass ceiling against the masculine.

This modern day feminine clergy intellectually chews the cud of heaven's authority while she rebukes and segregates Bible scriptures, which do not translate or interpret in kind to her and to the splinters of the congregations. Hence, Biblical truths are rejected while she teaches on doctrines of fog, emotions, feelings, and God's love **devoid** of God's laws and commandments. She alone knows what is good for God as she is propped and jockeyed into the logistics of the techno-plastic secular Church and her **adopted version** of "In-Christ."

Page 66
Da Vinci's Art…and
the Biblical Feminine Physics

Galatians 4:16…Am I therefore become your enemy, because I tell you the truth?

As End Time approaches it will become extremely, extremely difficult for the deceived feminine to cast out demons because the apostate church boosts up women appointed by men, and not of God. Also, God **will not allow** the homosexual spirit of clergy to cast out any demons or perform any exorcisms within society, because the Bible cannot be modified. It is spiritually dangerous for the church to prostrate the details of the devil while politically jockeying for the rights to exhibit the robes, the gender, the power, and authority of the Divine Throne of God.

Furthermore, the present day **apostate** church, regardless of the feminine factors and of course, the masculine factors, will be damaged greatly because they are so intertwined with politics and **sex supremacy** and with their own perceived grandeur; utilizing the LORD Jesus as a worldly commodity and a Worldwide Credit Card.

*Matthew 10:34…Think not that I am come to send peace on earth: I came not to send peace, but a **sword**.*

Leonard da Vinci…and the Homosexual Factors

The Homosexual Charges of Da Vinci… Hence, No Evidence

Most of Leonardo Da Vinci's spiritual masterpieces depict, embody, and encompass the ***Feminine Physics*** of the earth, the sequential, bone and flesh of the **masculine**.

It has been stated that Da Vinci hid **alleged** homosexual tendencies in his Art, it is especially alluded to his painting of the Mona Lisa. For centuries it has been claimed that Da Vinci painted the Mona Lisa disguised as himself in the likeness of the feminine gender. First and Foremost Leonardo was never found guilty of the sins of homosexuality; and the mystery and current evidence in the painting of the Mona Lisa is more of a cosmological nature, and properties thereof.

Da Vinci was also an honorable man. In today's modern era he is highly misunderstood and branded as a heretic and labeled as a homosexual, all based on deceptions.

Leonard da Vinci…and the Homosexual Factors

Leonardo da Vinci, was an introvert who kept to himself, he was a lone sparrow that God nurtured. Da Vinci was a gifted genius whose spiritual and scientific **mind** reached for the stars, but his inheritance and environment kept him in spiritual shackles.

*The silent images of Leonardo da Vinci's holy works of art are the **genuine testimonies** of his spiritual integrity and beliefs.*

It is probable that Leonardo da Vinci's stigma of illegitimacy coupled with his Biblical understanding of scriptures and God's laws and commandments, that shaped his character and demeanor to a more reclusive and introversive humble man.

These private and retiring qualities perhaps gave way to the false accusations of homosexuality. Based on the foundational evidence of the Biblically meaning and messages of his paintings, Da Vinci could **NOT** have been homosexual, nor, could he have dishonored himself and God with a hidden portrayal of self-incrimination of homosexual tendencies.

Leonard da Vinci…and the Homosexual Factors

Leonardo knew Bible scriptures, and the repercussions of God's curse for illegitimacy; for example, the Bastard Curse of Lot's daughters; origin of Moab; Genesis 19:35. Also knowing the Bible as he did, Da Vinci must have known that "**Eros Love**" is the only **sexual** love provided by the Spirit of God and reserved explicitly for a Husband and Wife, becoming one FLESH.

Reference Bastard Curse:
Genesis 19:35, 36…
And they made their father drink wine that night also: and the younger arose, and lay with him; and he perceived not when she lay down, nor when she arose. 36 Thus were both the daughters of Lot with child by their father.

Homosexuality
Scripture Reference
Romans 1:25,26,27,28…kjv
Who changed the truth of God into a lie, and worshipped and served the creature more than the Creator, who is blessed for ever. Amen.

Leonard da Vinci…and the Homosexual Factors

Romans 1:25,26,27,28 CONTINUED………

26 For this cause God gave them up unto vile affections: for even their women did change the natural use into that which is against nature: 27 And likewise also the men, leaving the natural use of the woman, burned in their lust one toward another; men with men working that which is unseemly, and receiving in themselves that recompense of their error which was meet. 28 And even as they did not like to retain God in their knowledge, God gave them over to a reprobate mind, to do those things which are not convenient;

Da Vinci personally experienced the stigma and fate that awaits immorality, especially that of homosexuality and its stinging attack against God's "ORDER" and society.. In light of his spiritual works of art, it is evident that Da Vinci clearly understood the mysteries of the Logos of God, i.e. **THOUGHT,** and the **PHYSIOLOGY of MARRIAGE** within the spiritual mind of the fallen Masculine and Feminine; and physics thereof.

Discernment:
God's Physiology of Marriage; The <u>Left Brain</u> and <u>Right Brain</u> of Creation Science:

The Physiology of Marriage between a Man and Woman is embedded in the genetics of Creation Science; the science of marriage is **greater** in the physics of **thought**, and less in **gender**. The sanctity of a Biblical Marriage is the exclusive inheritance of the Masculine and the Feminine.

Spiritually, the Left Brain ownership of the **Masculine** and his inherent characteristics is vowed in marriage to the Right Brain ownership of the **Feminine** with her inherent characteristics, hence, physics thereof…….equals **The Bookends of Marriage;** the ***thought*** of creation science. Scientifically and spiritually all human beings think with only 10% of the entire brain; 90% is not available to mankind. Our thoughts are interconnect with the universe; the universe has an equation of 99.999999999% physics of "**thought and wisdom**."

Page 72
The Physiology of Marriage…, between the Masculine and Feminine within the LOGOS

The Bible's Heterosexual marriage unifies the origin of **"_thought_"** processes and harmony with God; which is the Brain's functional physics of the **Logos**, logic and emotions within divine structure of reasoning.

Discernment:

1-   Biblically, the physics of the <u>Left Brain</u> equals the spiritual "Masculine Order."

2-   Biblically, the physics of the <u>Right Brian</u> equals the spiritual " Feminine Order."

Genetically, Creation Science clings and coheres only to a holy marriage of the Masculine and the Feminine; Logos Physics.

The Physiology of Marriage…, between the Masculine and Feminine within the LOGOS

DISCERNMENT CONTINUED…

Divine Physics of Marriage:

*The **LEFT BRAIN** properties and "thought" equations of the masculine…,WITH…, the **RIGHT BRAIN** properties and "thought" equations of the feminine.*

The physiology of marriage is beyond the sexual gift of a husband and wife. Spiritually and scientifically the physiology of marriage began in the Garden of Eden.

God gave mankind the power of "thought and reason;" but in a marriage "thought and reason" also becomes **ONE UNION**, Left Brain properties of the masculine married to the Right Brian properties of a feminine; like a child's active seesaw, it is never grounded. It balances the scales of both hemispheres of male and female for a lifetime of marriage, raising a family with complete wisdom and understanding of God's logic and balance.

The Physiology of Marriage…, between the Masculine and Feminine within the LOGOS

The Perils of Same-Sex Marriage in Homosexuality

Scientifically and spiritually, a man thinks with the power and dominance of his Left Brian; the left hemisphere of a man's brain has specific and difference characteristics of physics and "*thought*" processes.

Genetically, a man married to another man equals the same "*thought*" equations and patterns of the mind; hence, **TWO LEFT BRAINS** in the marriage; hindering human unity of God's logic and nature's harmony, hence, Biblical curse.

The Perils of Same-Sex Marriage in Lesbians

Scientifically and spiritually, a woman thinks with the power and dominance of her Right Brian; the Right hemisphere of a female's brain also has specific and difference characteristics of physics and thinking processes; the feminine is the complete opposite in the hemispheric properties of "**thought and reason**" from the man.

The Physiology of Marriage…, between the Masculine and Feminine within the LOGOS

CONTINUED…

The Perils of Same-Sex Marriage in Lesbians:

Genetically, a woman married to another woman equals the same "*thought*" equations and patterns of the mind; hence, **TWO RIGHT BRIANS** in marriage… hindering and weakening the origin of "*thought*," attacking God's laws and oneness which renders a spiritual curse.

The difference between mankind's *thoughts* and God's "*thoughts*," are that our way of thinking dwells in the Spiritual War of the earth; our thinking and reasoning is limited to the earth. The Lord's "*thoughts*" originate in the Third (3rd) Heaven; heaven is not contaminated with **SIN;** heaven's "***divine thoughts***" are 99.999999999% and man's inherent power of "*thought*" on the earth is only 10% of the MIND. Mankind is missing **90% of the "power of *thought*"** because God is the sovereign rule of the cosmos; the thinker of the universe.

Isaiah 55:8,9…kjv
For my thoughts are not your thoughts, neither are your ways my ways, saith the LORD. For as the heavens are higher than the earth, so are my ways higher than your ways, and my thoughts than your thoughts.

The Physiology of Marriage…, between the Masculine and Feminine within the LOGOS

The Renaissance Era did not dwell on the science physiology of the brain, of course, because it was not available to them; <u>But</u> the Renaissance Era thoroughly understood the Biblical ramifications of the "**<u>Logos,</u>**" the thinker; properties of God.

Before the <u>Feminine</u> and the <u>Masculine</u> fell out of grace with God, the structure and functions of the mind were of one divine physics. In *Genesis 5:2,* the Masculine and the Feminine were both called <u>ADAM</u>. After the origin of sin and God's curse to the earth ensued, Adam gave the woman, the feminine, her name; Adam then named her Eve; **before sin they were one**.

Genesis 5:2…Male and female created he them; and blessed them, and called their name Adam, in the day when they were created.

Genesis 3:6…And when the woman saw that the tree was good for food, and that it was pleasant to the eyes, and a tree to be desired to make one wise, she took of the fruit thereof, and did eat, and gave also unto her husband with her; and he did eat.

Genesis 3:20… And Adam called his wife's name Eve; because she was the mother of all living.

The Physiology of Marriage…, between the Masculine and Feminine within the **LOGOS**

The Masculine and Feminine… Spiritual MODES OF THINKING:

Left Brain Properties	Right Brian Properties
Black and White	Color
Logical	Random
Sequential	Intuitive
Analytical	Synthesizing
Critical Thinking	Creative Thinking
Linear	Non-linear
Objective	Subjective
Mathematical	Imagination
Rational	Emotional
Reasoning	Mystical
Intellect	Intuition
Analytic	Holistic
Parts	Wholes
Digital	Analogical
Dominates	Submit
Accuracy	Aesthetics

The Physiology of Marriage…, between the Masculine and Feminine within the LOGOS

A Marriage of the masculine and the feminine brings the two natural modes of physics and focus of the brain together. The Left Brain married to the Right Brain is the spiritual mandate and inheritance of **"thought."**

The Masculine and the Feminine are the only species on the earth that has the inherent intricacies of God's **origin of thought.**

The Predominant Biblical Science of the Masculine and Feminine Physics is… *"for the man is not of the woman; but the woman of the man."*

*After the first sin in the Garden of Eden, the mind of man was spiritual <u>realigned to include and process the knowledge of Evil within the physics</u> of **thoughts.***

The Physiology of Marriage…
The Bible's Feminine and Masculine Order

The Renaissance and the Bible's Feminine Physics

The Physics of the Biblical Feminine within God's Masculine "ORDER"

*The Renaissance Artists knew God's **Order of the Feminine**, the Science of Eve; the Physics and the blessings and consequences thereof.*

To best UNDERSTAND the crucial importance of God's Gender "Order" of Marriage, we must look directly into a Christian wedding of the Masculine and the Feminine on the earth; God's blueprint of his mandate. The "Order of the Feminine" never leaves the fortress of the Masculine..

A Wedding Day Under Grace; "In Christ:"

On this typical wedding day the feminine never leaves the *HANDS* of the masculine. The Virgin Bride walks down the aisle, *in the hand,* of her masculine father; her authority; Joshua 24:15.

Page 80
The Physiology of Marriage…
The Bible's Feminine and Masculine Order

While marching down the aisle the Bride sees her groom in the distance, awaiting. As the Bride and her father approach the groom, her father gives her **_hand to the masculine_** husband to be.

Once the Bride is separated from her father, the masculine and the feminine, "In-Christ," step forwards to the realm of the sacred altar; the masculine Throne of God; the epitome of the Third (3rd.) Heaven on earth. **The Virgin Bride in the purity of white,** *the presences of all color*, and the Groom in his black, *the absence of all color,* begin their verbal covenant to God; creator of the heavens and the earth.

In the presence of God and the sanctity of the Church, the masculine authority of God and the Holy Spirit join the couple in a ceremonious marriage with their vows to God; the feminine and the masculine become **ONE FLESH**.

Hence, the family "In-Christ" rears the feminine; Biblically, from a child to a maiden, the **FEMININE** never leaves the hand of the masculine, because **she is genetically and spiritually of the man**.

Page 81
The Physiology of Marriage…
The Bible's Feminine and Masculine Order

The Renaissance knew the "ORDER" of the Feminine Physics.

Da Vinci and some of the Renaissance Master Artists introduced visual wisdom of the Bible's Feminine Factors, under-the-law. Another notable and gifted Master Artist was Antonello da Messina; this Renaissance Master Artist from Sicily also gave meanings and messages of the semblances of the feminine and the masculine, under-the-law. Two of Antonello da Messina's most famous compositions are that of **The Virgin Annunciate** and **Portrait of a Man.**

Reference Scriptures:

Genesis 2:22…kjv
And the rib, which the LORD God had taken from man, made he a woman, and brought her unto the man.

<u>The Family "in Christ"</u> *Reference Scriptures:*
Joshua 24:15…kjv
And if it seem evil unto you to serve the LORD, choose you this day whom ye will serve; whether the gods which your fathers served that were on the other side of the flood, or the gods of the Amorites, in whose land ye dwell: <u>but as for me and my house, we will serve the LORD.</u>

The Physiology of Marriage…
The Bible's Feminine and Masculine Order

Genesis 2:22…kjv

And the rib, which the LORD God had taken from man, made he a woman, and brought her unto the man. 23 And Adam said, this is now bone of my bones, and flesh of my flesh: She shall be called Woman, because she was taken out of Man.

Marriage

Reference Scripture:

John 2:1. 2…kjv

And the third day there was a marriage in Cana of Galilee; and the mother of Jesus was there: 2 And both Jesus was called, and his disciples, to the marriage.

Ephesians 5:22, 23…kjv

Wives, submit yourselves unto your own husbands, as unto the Lord. 23 For the husband is the head of the wife, even as Christ is the head of the church: and he is the saviour of the body.

The Last Supper…
Da Vinci's Biblically Encoded Composition

The Biblical Mystery of the Last Supper…….
<u>CROSSROADS</u> of Law and Grace

The Last Supper…
Da Vinci's Biblically Encoded Composition

The Mystery of the Last Supper; <u>Crossroads</u> of Law and Grace

Why has Leonardo da Vinci's composition of "The Last Supper" been so intriguing and mysterious? Because, it's a magnificent depiction of the Biblical crossroads of **Law and Grace,** grace and mercy **awaiting** the next day. The Last Supper is the threefold apex of the physical Law, and the road toward Grace and Salvation pending… **nigh**. The composite depicts heaven's crossroads which was the pivotal turning point before the gift of salvation; juncture thereof.

There are several factors that come to mind at this pivotal and historical Biblical time frame. First and foremost, Leonardo da Vinci establishes the visual crossroads of <u>LAW</u> and <u>GRACE</u> in the painting; also it is the crossroads of death towards life, because Jesus was to be crucified the very next day with the betrayal of Judas Iscariot. It was the last time Jesus and all of his disciples communed together.

The Last Supper…
Da Vinci's Biblically Encoded Composition

The Biblical Crossroads…the very next day, the earth would be released from bondage of the LAW with the shedding of his blood; and water. The very next day, the temple's veil would rent in half, releasing mankind from centuries under-the-law and into the dispensation of Grace, salvation; the soul's eternal life; and the very next day the earth did quake, and the rocks rent.

Leonardo da Vinci had the wisdom of Bible scriptures and sequence thereof, because The Last Supper depicts multiple panoramic Biblical scriptural codes within the dimensional and perspectives of the composition.

In The Last Supper, the evidence renders truths that Leonardo da Vinci did not have **heretical or renegade** beliefs as alleged and suggested in Dan Brown's Novel, "The Da Vinci Code;" or the allegations that the CHURCH ordered the cover-up of Mary Magdalene's role as the Holy Grail. Da Vinci was a Christian who respected and honored God undeniably, the truth is evident based on the merits of his spiritual works of Art. He had a unique way of illustrating the divine mysterious of God and a transcendental capacity of understanding the wisdom of the Bible. Scriptures, and Codes.

The Last Supper…
Da Vinci's Biblical Encoded Composition

*Like the layers of an **onion**, "The Last Supper" has numerous layers and layers of Biblical messages, scriptural meanings within Renaissance codes.*

<u>The Last Supper</u>
Scripture Reference:

<u>Mark 14:22 - 24…kjv</u>
And as they did eat, Jesus took bread, and blessed, and brake it, and gave to them, and said, Take, eat: this is my body. 23 And he took the cup, and when he had given thanks, he gave it to them: and they all drank of it. 24 And he said unto them, This is my blood of the new testament, which is shed for many.

<u>Matthew 26:27-29…kjv</u>
And he took the cup, and gave thanks, and gave it to them, saying, Drink ye all of it; 28For this is my blood of the New Testament, which is shed for many for the remission of sins. 29 But I say unto you, I will not drink henceforth of this fruit of the vine, until that day when I drink it new with you in my Father's kingdom.

The Last Supper…
Da Vinci's Biblical Encoded Composition

Reference Scriptures:

Veil of the Temple

Reference Scripture:

Matthew 27:51…kjv

And, behold, the veil of the temple was rent in twain from the top to the bottom; and the earth did quake, and the rocks rent;

Mark 15:38…kjv

And the veil of the temple was rent in twain from the top to the bottom.

Luke 23:45…kjv

And the sun was darkened, and the veil of the temple was rent in the midst.

Iscariot Betrayal

Reference Scripture:

Matthew 26:21…kjv

And as they did eat, he said, Verily I say unto you, that one of you shall betray me.

Decoding…The Biblical Mystery of Da Vinci's Last Supper

<u>Bible Messages, Scriptural Meaning, and Codes</u>:

Leonardo da Vinci's composition of The Last Supper is encoded and condensed with visual scriptural meaning, messages, codes and perspectives of the Genesis 3:15.

Genesis 3:15…"SEED of the <u>WOMAN</u>."

Leonardo da Vinic painted this spiritual composition with the code of the Womb of Woman, the feminine physics of the earth; from the origin of the fallen Eve and the curse that God gave the serpent. Da Vinci encoded the scriptural message of the Womb of Genesis 3:15. Da Vinci's composite encodes the antecedent of God's curse to the serpent.

The Ancient Symbol **V**

*The depiction of the ancient letter **V** in Da Vinci painting is the sacred womb……the Biblical code that will bruise the serpent's head.*

The Last Supper depicts the three fold completion of Genesis 3:15… And I will put enmity between thee and the woman, and between thy seed and her seed; it shall bruise thy head, and thou shalt bruise his heel.

One must remember that in the Spiritual War, Satan attempted to interrupt the "Seed of the Woman" in several crucial Biblical turning points; **Satan**, *continuously tried to block the seed in the virgin,* **" WOMB OF WOMAN,"** *from coming forth to the earth.*

The Last Supper…, Da Vinci's Biblical Encoded Composition

Furthermore, Da Vinci's composite of The Last Supper is depicted in the fullness of time of the "LAW;" all of the powers and the dominant rule of the law were still in effect. Jesus was born under-the-law; Jesus was made of woman under-the-law…;

Galatians 4:4,5…But when the fullness of the time was come, God sent forth his Son, made of woman, made under the law, 5 to redeem them that were under the law, that we might receive the adoption of sons.

The Last Supper is **<u>Biblically</u>** encoded with the Genesis 3:15,…….. <u>Seed of Woman</u>, it is not a secret code of an alleged marriage and conspiracy of a bloodline with **<u>Jesus the Christ</u>** and Mary Magdalene; this is a misrepresentation and fabrication of the historical facts which is alleged in Dan Brown's novel, "The Da Vinci Code."

The Last Supper…,
Da Vinci's Biblical Encoded Composition

Da Vinci's "The Last Supper" depicts and encompasses Renaissance codes and messages of Biblical origins; it also illustrates visual perspectives of the Bible, scriptural codes, and pictorial revelations of the following wisdom:

1- God's Plan for Mankind's Salvation
2- The Numerical Codes of Spiritual Warfare
3- Authorities of SIX AND SEVEN
4- The Partitioned Codes of Good verses Evil
5- The Prince and Power of the Air; authority of
6- The Hebrew Day /Night Watches and Hours
7- Encoded Hues, Spiritual Color Spectrum
8- Blood in the Chalice or the Blood in the Vein
9- The semblance, Aura, of the Feminine Symbol of the *V*; the **Seed of Woman**

The Last Supper…,
Da Vinci's <u>Biblical</u> Encoded Composition

And………the Physics of the Fallen Eve; it encircles prophecy and manifestation of the historical events from The Old Testament to The New Testament, that of Genesis 3:15 to Matthew 1:20.

And………it encompasses The First Judgment, The Curse on the Devil, **The Curse of the Woman**, The Curse of the Land, The Curse of the Man and the Promise of the Redeemer.

Scripture Reference:

<u>Genesis 3:15</u>…*And I will put enmity between thee and the woman, and between thy seed and her seed; it shall bruise thy head, and thou shalt bruise his heel.*

<u>Matthew 1:20</u>…*But while he thought on these things, behold, the angel of the Lord appeared unto him in a dream, saying, Joseph, thou son of David, fear not to take unto thee Mary thy wife: for that which is conceived in her is of the Holy Ghost.*

Page 93
The Last Supper…,
Da Vinci's <u>Biblical</u> Encoded Composition

Da Vinci's painting, of "The Last Supper" has been thrust into the arena of doubt and with deception, disguised as truth; all in the most recent publication of Dan Brown's novel.

DOUBT: How does one feed an ANCIENT elephant (i.e. a *spiritual falsity*) to the population of the earth? The answer is…….a spoonful at a time, small daily intervals of deception, teaspoons of doubt everyday.

<u>Biblical Truths</u>:
…All Wisdom Comes From God
……All Deception Comes From Satan

The Ancient V Symbol

The **V** shape "connection" in the painting is Da Vinci's portrayal of the God's Genesis curse and physics of the Feminine Seed that would cut down the serpent, bruise his head; Curse of Genesis 3:15 ordered by God.

Page 94
The Last Supper…,
Da Vinci's <u>Biblical</u> Encoded Composition

Da Vinci did not depict the symbol of the **V** for the sacred feminine, which Dan Brown alleges to be Mary Magdalene. The ancient **V** symbol in the painting is the **<u>representation</u>** of the Genesis 3:15 WOMAN;. The symbol represents the physical fulfillment and presence of Jesus Christ who was born of the feminine seed. The letter **V** symbol is the **<u>visual illustration</u>** of the vessel of woman, the seed of the woman who would bring forth the redeemer, through the powers of the Holy Spirit; **<u>THE VIRGIN WOMB</u>** that would bruise the serpent's head.

In Dan Brown's novel, "The Da Vinci Code." it alleges that Da Vinci secretly encoded the symbol of the letter **V** to depict the Holy Grail that of Mary Magdalene with child; this is an attack against the Core of Christianity. This is a hoax and deception, because the earth has been waiting for generations upon generations for the <u>WOMB of the WOMAN</u> spoken in Genesis 3:15 throughout Matthew 1:20,

The Last Supper…,
Da Vinci's <u>Biblical</u> Encoded Composition

Leonardo da Vinci had a unique custom and style of using symbols and numerics to illustrate visually and condense the wisdom of the Biblical Curse of Genesis 3:15. the **<u>SACRED WOMAN AND HER SEED</u>**; her seed visually manifested through the palette and spectrum of color in Da Vinci's depiction of The Last Supper's holy composition.

Now, one must remember, that Da Vinci and some Renaissance Artists used Roman and ancient symbols and codes, to convey and simplify and also condense the total wisdom and understanding of Biblical events and factors in their spiritual composites.

There is not a woman in Da Vinci's painting of the Last Supper, as Dan Brown alleges, but only the **<u>representation</u>** of the Feminine Biblical message… that would bring forth the seed of salvation and eternal life.

John the disciple is the one to the left of the painting. The disciple John did not have a beard like the other eleven disciples because he was a very young man. The Renaissance Artist knew how to distinguish features of age and character. They had a unique talent and custom of portraying many facets and techniques for Biblical illustrations.

The Last Supper…,
Da Vinci's **Biblical** Encoded Composition

Decoding…The Ancient V Symbol

The **V** in the painting depicts the **Womb of Woman**, which was spoken and ordered by God and prophesied, the sacred woman, to conceive in her womb the seed from the Holy Ghost; the divine mandate of heaven. The **V** is the prelusion to the divine Savior and his physical manifestation from the seed of woman and from the origin of the **mother of all living**…,*Genesis 3:20*…*And Adam called his wife's name Eve; because she was the mother of all living.*

When one looks at Da Vinci's Last Supper from our visual perspective…, the person on the left of Jesus is John the disciple, **NOT** Mary Magdalene as it infers in Dan Brown's novel, "The Da Vinci Code."

John was a young lad, he loved Jesus profoundly; John the disciple was very young and he did not have facial hair. Da Vinci was a perfectionist and he had extreme discerning awareness of the profiles of each and every disciple of the Lord. John was beloved by Jesus; out of all the disciples John was the favorite of Jesus.

Page 97
The Last Supper...,
Da Vinci's <u>Biblical</u> Encoded Composition

John the disciple was entrusted with the Book of Revelations; he was also with Jesus in the Mount of Transfiguration; John was at the foot of the cross. Out of all the twelve disciples, John, was the only one who did not suffer a horrible death; he was blessed in his old age. Leonardo da Vinci knew all the qualities and facial features of John and Da Vinci knew that John was called the **<u>Beloved Disciple of Jesus</u>**. As stated, most of the Renaissance Artists had this custom of emphasizing and illustrating the tiny details and unique facets of the individual's distinguishing persona of Biblical accuracy.

Dan Brown alleges that Jesus had a child with Mary Magdalene and that their bloodline still exists today in the descendants of French Royalty; as the evidence will prove, this is totally erroneous. The mystery of the letter **V symbol in the painting,** between John the disciple and the Lord Jesus is a <u>Renaissance representation of the feminine physics</u>, the knowledge and wisdom of the **<u>Womb of Woman</u>**; the womb of woman *that* would bring forth the *Seed of Salvation*...in Genesis 3:15.

The Last Supper…,
Da Vinci's <u>Biblical</u> Encoded Composition

Scripture Reference:

Genesis 3:15…And I will put enmity between thee and the woman, and between thy seed and her seed; it shall bruise thy head, and thou shalt bruise his heel.

The Seed of Woman manifested in the flesh in Da Vinci's Last Supper's painting renders the complete visual and the perspective of Bible prophesy. Leonardo da Vinci painted and encoded facts and sequences of Biblical history.

<<<+>>>

The ancient symbol of the **<u>Feminine V,</u>** introduces Leonardo da Vinci's Biblical code and scriptural message of the **"<u>Seed of Woman;</u>"** the virgin womb that would bring forth the savior in the flesh.

Page 99
The Last Supper...,
Da Vinci's <u>Biblical</u> Encoded Composition

Decoding.......The <u>Dualistic</u> "V" in The Last Supper's Composition

*1- The Roman **<u>Numeral</u>** V, (5)*

*2- The Ancient Symbol of the feminine **<u>Letter</u>** V*

Decoding...The Roman Numeral Five:

Leonardo da Vinci also **<u>superimposed</u>** transparent ancient letters and numbers in the masterpiece in order to condense the maximum Biblical wisdom.

The Symbol *V* also has a dualistic representation of the spiritual number **<u>FIVE</u>**; Da Vinci used the number five from the Roman origin, *V*. The number **<u>FIVE</u>**, Biblically means GRACE and MERCY, the favor and goodness of God.

Page 100
The Last Supper…,
Da Vinci's <u>Biblical</u> *Encoded Composition*

In the Bible, God gave **FIVE** ministries to the world to reveal the Gospel; they are Apostles, Prophets, Evangelist, Pastors, and Teachers. John the disciple who is to the right of Jesus in the painting wrote **FIVE** books revealing God's wisdom; they are The Gospel of John, 1st John, 2nd John, 3rd John, and Revelation. Also, Moses was given the **FIVE** books of the Bible; origins.

The number five is also significant in the Holy Anointing Oil which had **FIVE** components; they were Olive Oil, Cassis, Calamus, Myrrh, and Cinnamon.

Furthermore, there were **FIVE** offerings on the Altar of Sacrifice; they were the Sin Offering, the Trespass Offering, the Burnt Offering, the Meat Offering, and Peace Offering. **FIVE** is also the number for **CHOICE,** Mankind's FREE-WILL.

Leonardo da Vinci used symbols, numerical codes, progressive panels, clusters of groups and groupings, hand gestures, color specifics, shade and light and various geometric and dimensional perspectives in order to maximize the Biblical <u>content</u> and <u>context</u> of God's mandates and Salvation's Journey.

The Last Supper…,
Da Vinci's <u>Biblical</u> Encoded Composition

Decoding……..*The Conversion of the Ancient Symbol of the Letter <u>**V**</u> into the Roman Numeral <u>**M**</u>…, Superimposed*

*The ancient symbol of the letter **V** is also transposed and superimposed into the Roman Numeral **M**.*

*The code of the letter **V** is utilized further by Da Vinci to transpose the localized geometrics into the Roman Numeral **M**. The Roman Numeral **M** encompasses John the disciple and Jesus. This numeral **M** is also Biblical in content.*

*Most of the misguided interpretations from "The Da Vinci Code Novel" infers that the Roman Numeral **M** stands for **<u>Mary Magdalene</u>** which is highly ludicrous, because for thousands of years the world has been waiting for the **<u>MESSIAH</u>**; rod of the stem of Jesse; Isaiah 11:1.*

The Last Supper…,
Da Vinci's Biblical Encoded Composition

Decoding…….
The Roman Numeral 1000, (M)

*The code of the transparent geometrics of the Roman Numeral **M**, means **Messiah** not Magdalene; the Roman Numeral **M** also interprets the equation of the numeric of ONE THOUSAND (1000). Leonardo da Vinci layered the Biblical wisdom of **One Day** with the Lord is as **One Thousand Years**, 2nd Peter 3:8.*

Reference Scripture
2nd Peter 3:8…But, beloved, be not ignorant of this one thing, that one day is with The Lord as a thousand years, and a thousand years as one day.

The evidence and meanings of the equations of letters and numbers are all Biblical in content.

The Last Supper…,
Da Vinci's <u>Biblical</u> Encoded Composition

***Decoding**……..The Roman Numeral 1000, (M):*

Da Vinci painted and illustrated wisdom in condensed layers, like the layers of an onion. If you remove the layers of an onion you still have an onion; the Last Supper has layers upon layers of condensed perspectives of explicit Biblical meanings and messages.

The illusion of the numeral *M* also encompasses and reveals Jesus as, **<u>the Alpha and the Omega</u>**, seated next to the writer of the Revelations; John the disciple was entrusted with the Book of Revelations, Omega means the ENDING.

Reference Scripture:
Revelation 1:8…kjv
I am Alpha and Omega, the beginning and the ending, saith the Lord, which is, and which was, and which is to come, the Almighty.

The Last Supper…,
Da Vinci's <u>Biblical</u> Encoded Composition

Decoding…The Last Supper's CEILING

<u>Biblical Prologue</u>:

Jesus came to earth to redeem us from the law, death, and bondage of sin and to break the strongholds of the powers of Satan. In spite of this, Satan is still the prince and power of the air. The territories of the prince of darkness dwell in the first (1st) and second (2nd) heaven; the earth is part of Satan's realm of authority.

Reference Scripture…
Ephesians 6:12…For we wrestle not against flesh and blood, but against principalities, against powers, against the rulers of the darkness of this world, against spiritual wickedness in high places.

$$((((((6))))))$$

Satan's numerical number is the SIX.
Satan is the prince and power of the AIR.
Satan is the accuser and the deceiver.

The Last Supper…,
Da Vinci's <u>Biblical</u> Encoded Composition

In the Last Supper's painting, the ceiling has an encoded numeric equation of the number Six, the prince of darkness, Satan.

Leonardo painted the ceiling with six ladders, they are black ladders in rows of six; the entire perspective of this ceiling was visually depicted and imaged directly over the head of Jesus. In the Bible we have the reference of Jacob's ladder. The Bible informs us of the spiritual powers of heaven's ladder.

Genesis 28:11,12,13…And he lighted upon a certain place, and tarried there all night, because the sun was set; and he took of the stones of that place, and put them for his pillows, and lay down in that place to sleep. 12 And he dreamed, and behold a ladder set up on the earth, and the top of it reached to heaven: and behold the angels of God ascending and descending on it. 13 And, behold, the LORD stood above it, and said, I am the LORD God of Abraham thy father, and the God of Issac: the Land whereon thou liest, to thee will I give it, and to they seed;

Now, Jacob saw these angels on a divine ladder ascending and descending, but Satan's ladders are black. Lucifer was a divine angel; Lucifer was an archangel of God before he was cut to the ground for pride and arrogance; Isaiah 14:12.

The Last Supper…,
Da Vinci's <u>Biblical</u> Encoded Composition

Isaiah 14:12…How art thou fallen from heaven, O Lucifer, son of the morning! How art thou cut down to the ground, which didst weaken the nations!

Here we have Da Vinci illustrating black ladders above the seated center of Jesus. Leonardo, of course, knew that Satan used to be an angel of God. The Renaissance Era absolutely knew that Lucifer is a **<u>FALLEN ANGEL</u>**, with the numeric of Six.

Da Vinci, centered the numeric of the SIX directly over the presence of Jesus; the square radius of the ceiling barely encompass his twelve disciples; this illusion projects and simulates most of the disciples away and into the geometric of the outer walls. The SIX squared radius of the ceiling has its total emphasis above the Lord; six ladders.

This ceiling is painted and focused directly above the centered image of Jesus; remarkably the disciples share the SAME SPACE of the ceiling, YET, they are projected away from the immediate radius and position of this numeric ceiling, but the projection of the **<u>SIX-LADDER CEILING</u>** only has its focus above Jesus Christ.

Page 107
The Last Supper…,
Da Vinci's <u>Biblical</u> Encoded Composition

Da Vinci transposed Satan's spiritual codes into the geometric structure of the Last Supper's composites.

Da Vinci **<u>also</u>** superimposed Lucifer's spiritual equations in the structured symmetry of the geometry.

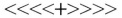

Scripture Reference:

<u>Satan's Powers</u>

Ephesians 6:12…kjv

For we wrestle not against flesh and blood, but against principalities, against powers, against the rulers of the darkness of this world, against spiritual wickedness in high places.

<u>The Creature Among Us</u>

Romans 1:25…kjv

Who changed the truth of God into a lie, and worshipped and served the creature more than the Creator, who blessed for ever. Amen.

The Last Supper…,
Da Vinci's <u>Biblical</u> Encoded Composition

<u>Scripture Reference:</u>

ORIGIN……. LUCIFER

Ezekiel 28:13,14,15…kjv

Thou hast been in Eden the Garden of God; every precious stone was thy covering, the sardius, topaz, and the diamond, the beryl, the onyx, and the jasper, the sapphire, the emerald, and the carbuncle, and gold: the workmanship of they tabrets and of they pipes was prepared in thee in the day that thou was created. 14 thou art the anointed cherub that covereth; and I have set thee so: thou wast upon the holy mountain of God; thou hast walked up and down in the midst of the stones of fire.

<u>Isaiah 14:12, 13,14…kjv</u>

How art thou fallen from heaven, O Lucifer, son of the morning! how art thou cut down to the ground, which didst weaken the nations! 13 For thou hast said in thine heart, I will ascend into heaven, I will exalt my throne above the stars of God: I will sit also upon the mount of the congregation, in the sides of the north: 14 I will ascend above the heights of the clouds; I will be like the most High.

The Last Supper…,
Da Vinci's Biblical Encoded Composition

Decoding… The Last Supper 's WALLS

Biblical Prologue:

In Leonardo da Vinci's personal notes, he wrote about the science of darkness and how it dominates the science of light. These notes capture the essential understanding of the **Physical darkness** and light…; and the **Spiritual darkness** and light.

The physical and the spiritual properties of darkness and light interconnect in the Book of Genesis when God separated the light from the darkness…;

Genesis 1:3, 4…And God said, Let there be light: and there was light. 4 And God saw the light, that it was good: and God divided the light from the darkness; origin.

The Last Supper…,
Da Vinci's <u>Biblical</u> Encoded Composition

Decoding…THE WALLS

In the Last Supper, Leonardo, gives **<u>Light</u>** to the right side of the walls……But, to the left side of the walls he illustrates **<u>Darkness.</u>** The encoded panoramic format and structure of the walls and panels renders the apparent depth and recession of the day the progression of the night.

Da Vinci used the format of panels to separate the daytime from the night. He painted receding geometric panels on the walls of the Last Supper's composition. The illustration of panels for Da Vinci was a method of establishing TIME, such as a place in TIME, or TIME itself as a clock. Leonardo da Vinci illustrated TIME by positioning panels within the space of the walls.

The references of panels are also mentioned in one of Da Vinci's commissioned paintings for The Confraternity of the Immaculate Conception of which a mysterious controversy developed with the directives of the subject matter of the painting. The depictions of the panels were specified in the contract; this contract was to include and depict <u>God in the overhead</u> and two side panels depicting two prophets.

The Last Supper…,
Da Vinci's <u>Biblical</u> Encoded Composition

The contract also specified that the <u>Virgin of the Rocks</u> would be the centerpiece. However, these specifics were never to be, because Da Vinci deviated from the original specifications of depicting God in the overhead and the prophets in separate panels of identity.

As in The Last Supper, Da Vinci used panels for specifications of sequences of "**TIME FACTORS**" of historical Biblical events and prophecies. In other words, Da Vinci, used the analogical question of……. *"What came first? The Chicken or the Egg"?*

Da Vinci was a man of discerning God's logic of directives of the past, the present, the future and painting the progressive pace of God's Orders and manifestations of God's mandates.

For Da Vinci, to paint one prophet to the left panel and one prophet to the right panel at random, probably would have been an unfocused and unbalanced truth.

The Last Supper…, Da Vinci's <u>Biblical</u> Encoded Composition

Without the sequences of God's Logos, "*thought*," what the Confraternity was requesting of Leonardo would have been a *Helter-Skelter composite*; hence, Da Vinci was a perfectionist to the exact order of God's directives. As his paintings reveal, Da Vinci's Biblical knowledge and wisdom was probably beyond the discerning abilities of the Confraternity of the Immaculate Conception as to the Bible's sequential protocol towards a **visual** Biblical layout; culminating into a condensed divine composition.

The mystery and controversy over the commissioned contract of the Confraternity of the Immaculate Conception and Da Vinci is centered on a disagreement with the commissioned authenticity and how God's mandates were *EXCECUTED* in the Bible in reference to the layout of the painting; and Leonardo da Vinci had the superior wisdom and discernment of the Confraternity's subject matter, because the two versions of the Madonna (s) of the Rocks are in precise accuracy of the sequential Logos of God. Da Vinci was a perfectionist to the smallest details of Biblical progression of time.

The Last Supper…,
Da Vinci's **Biblical** Encoded Composition

The Mystery Panels, the Metaphors of the Hebrew Reckoning of Day & Night… [Watches & Hours]

The mystery of the Panels on the walls in the Last Supper's composition indicate and illustrate the reckoning of day and night; watches and hours.

*The Last Supper's walls from right… to… left, are encoded with a Biblical metaphor and perspective of the **HEBREW WATCHES AND HOURS** of the day and of the night. The geometric perspective of the panels progressively **adjourn**, recess, the ending of the day to the right and the ending of the night to the left.*

*In the Last Supper, the **PANELS OF THE WALLS** depict metaphorically, the Hebrew Watches and Hours.*

Da Vinci, illustrated FOUR PANELS to the RIGHT of the walls, and another FOUR PANELS to the LEFT of the walls.

Page 114
The Last Supper…,
Da Vinci's <u>Biblical</u> Encoded Composition

The Last Supper has a total of EIGHT PANELS;

1-   Four panels for the light of day…and
2-   Four panels for the darkness of the night

((((DAY HOURS))))

Da Vinci depicts FOUR PANELS to portray the New Testament's Watches. To the right of the composition Leonardo, paints FOUR PANELS for the **Hebrew Day Hours**; each panel represents a code of three hours per panel.

The Day Hours, are to the right of The Last Supper, where Da Vinci enhances the radiance of the LIGHT.

The Third Hour of the Day………..9:00 a.m.
The Sixth Hour of the Day……….12:00 midday
The Ninth Hour of the Day……….3:00 p.m.
The Twelfth Hour of the Day……..6:00 p.m.

(It's three hours per panel, = equaling 12 hours.)

The Last Supper…,
Da Vinci's <u>Biblical</u> Encoded Composition

*In essence, the wall panels of the Last Supper's composition, also transfigures the perspectives of ………***the 24 Hour Clock***; "Time," itself.*

<u>Reference Scriptures on the Four Day Hours:</u>

Matthew 20:3…And he went out about the third hour and saw others standing idle in the marketplace,

Acts of the Apostles 2:15…For these are not drunken, as ye suppose, seeing it is but the third hour of the day.

Luke 23:44…And it was about the sixth hour, and there was a darkness over all the earth until the ninth hour.

Page 116
The Last Supper…,
Da Vinci's <u>Biblical</u> Encoded Composition

((((NIGHT))))

THE NIGHT WATCHES:

The **Night Watches** are to the left of the Last Supper where Leonardo da Vinci introduces the dimness into the DARKNESS; heavy obscurity.

The Adoption of the Greek and Roman division of the <u>NIGHT</u> fell into twelve hours of <u>FOUR WATCHES</u>.

First Night Watch
The Evening was……………6:00p.m. to 9:00p.m.

Second Night Watch
The Midnight was………… 9:00p.m. to 12:00a.m.

Third Night Watch
The Cock-Crowing was…… 12:00a.m. to 3:00a.m.

Fourth Night Watch
The Morning was……………3:00a.m. to 6:00a.m.

(It was three hours per <u>WATCH</u>, equaling 12 hours.)

Page 117
The Last Supper…,
Da Vinci's Biblical Encoded Composition

Jesus is the New Testament

Reference Scriptures on the Four Night Watches:

Matthew 14:25, 26…And in the fourth watch of the night Jesus went unto them, walking on the sea. 26 And when the disciples saw him walking on the sea, they were troubled, saying, It is a spirit; and they cried out for fear.

Mark 13:35…Watch ye therefore: for ye know not when the master of the house cometh, at even, or at midnight, or at the cock crowing, or in the morning:

Luke 12:38…And if he shall come in the second watch, or come in the third watch, and find them so, blessed are those servants.

$$((((+))))$$

These were the Watches and Hours that Leonardo da Vinci illustrated with the panels on the walls of the Last Supper, but however, before the New Testament the **ANCIENT HEBREW NIGHT & DAY** was divided into **THREE** watches instead of FOUR.

The Last Supper…,
Da Vinci's <u>Biblical</u> Encoded Composition

Decoding… The Last Supper's DISCIPLES

<u>Biblical Prologue:</u>

In the composition of The Last Supper, Jesus and his twelve disciples were still under the dominant powers of the Law.
Reference scripture:
Galatians 4:4, 5….But when the fullness of the time was come, God sent forth his Son, made of a woman, made under the law, To redeem them that were under the law, that we might receive the adoption of sons.

In The Last Supper, the dividing point of the painting is not Jesus, **although he is centered…….**; **the dividing point of the painting is the ancient symbol of the letter V**.

The Symbol of the ancient letter **V**, is also a **Dualistic Code**, a Renaissance code with two separate perspectives; Bible wisdom.

Page 119
The Last Supper…,
Da Vinci's <u>Biblical</u> *Encoded Composition*

<u>The Dualistic Code:</u>

Here again, the ancient Symbol **V** encodes the Womb of Woman; seed of woman that would bring forth the savior, Genesis 3:15; the representation of the feminine factor.

AND

The ancient Symbol **V** also separates the Supper Table numerically. The letter **V** separates visually **<u>Six Men</u>** from **<u>Seven Men</u>** which are spiritual numbers; in the numeric of the Spiritual War, Satan is a six and God is a seven. Also the **V** symbol in the painting, separates the representation, *<u>metaphor</u>*, of the three-way curse of **<u>enmity</u>**. The symbol divides the curse of "**<u>enmity</u>**" to the left and righteousness to the right. To the left of the horizontal plane, the dagger is revealed and the seed of woman is asymmetrical to the right; messages and meanings.

This code illustrates a dual visual perspective of the composition's Biblical wisdom. This symbol allowed Leonardo da Vinci to skillfully and ingeniously, condense the scriptural wisdom of the Bible.

The Last Supper…,
Da Vinci's <u>Biblical</u> Encoded Composition

By separating six men from seven men, with the symbol of the letter **V**, Da Vinci was able to portray and allude to the root and illusion of……..*ENMITY*. The dagger in the painting is portrayed to the left of the symbol **V,** and the dagger is positioned on the supper table between Peter and Judas Iscariot. **<u>The Enmity of Genesis 3:15.</u>**

$$((((((SEED\ OF\ WOMAN))))))$$

<u>THE LEFT of the V:</u>

Across the Supper Table, the allusion and numeric of <u>*ENMITY*</u> *is depicted to the left of the symbol V. The left of the symbol V, follows the six men into the darkness.*

<u>The Disciples to the Left of the **V:**</u>

John, Peter, Judas Iscariot, Andrew, James the less, and Bartholomew; a total of six.

The Last Supper…,
Da Vinci's <u>Biblical</u> Encoded Composition

THE RIGHT of the V:

The right side of the symbol V, follows a numerical count of seven men into the light of the composition's walls. The right side of the symbol V renders authority to the divine number seven of The Lord God.

The Lord Jesus, **Plus** Six Disciples are to the Right of the V:

*The **<u>Numerical Equation</u>** to the right of the symbol V, is a visual grouping of God's number **<u>SEVEN</u>**. Leonardo da Vinci depicts and separates the authority of the number SEVEN in the realm of the following men:*

Jesus, Thomas, James the Elder, Philip, Matthew, Thaddaeus, and Simon……Heaven's Number Seven Encoded.

The Last Supper…,
Da Vinci's <u>Biblical</u> Encoded Composition

*Across the Supper Table, Da Vinci, illustrates the Spiritual War's numeric of six and seven and their perspectives from the pivotal **<u>Asymmetrical</u>** positioning of the Symbol V in the painting; the Womb of Woman segregates six men from seven men.*

<u>The Mystery of the Horizontal Supper Table and the Symbol V</u>:

1- **<u>Six</u>** men to the left of the horizontal table, towards… the code of darkness

2- **<u>Seven</u>** men to the right of the horizontal table, towards… the code of light

*In the Last Supper's composition, the horizontal seating arrangement of the twelve disciples, enabled Leonardo da Vinci to masterfully **<u>condense</u>** the wisdom of the Spiritual War's equation of numbers and the scriptural wisdom of the curse of Genesis 3:15.*

The Last Supper...,
Da Vinci's <u>Biblical</u> Encoded Composition

What is the Mystery of the Number Twelve?...God is Masculine.

In the Last Supper, the Masculine of TWELVE disciples, enforces the "Order of Heaven;" the Physics of the MASCULINE.

In this painting, Da Vinci, illustrates groups of three for each quarter of a twelve hour day. God authorizes "Time" and God is masculine. "Time," was created by God. The Logos existed before of Space and Time and the foundations of the universe.

Leonardo da Vinci also emphasized the <u>MASCULINE ORDER</u> of the third Heaven with the twelve disciples. He grouped the twelve disciples in the "Hebrew Order" of the Twelve Hour Day. In the painting, when one positions the Lord Jesus as the pivotal indicator of the point of "Time," the mystery of the clock is revealed with six hours to the right and six hours to the left in the representation of men. The twelve disciples are the physical analogy of the hours of the day.

The Last Supper…,
Da Vinci's Biblical Encoded Composition

Decoding… The Last Supper's WINDOWS

Biblical Prologue:

Da Vinci's codes in the Last Supper also have a focus and illustration of three windows behind the Lord Jesus. These three windows are analogical and metaphorical in the nature of interpretation. The knowledge of the Artist is to overlap multiple visual Bible wisdom, like layers of an onion. There again, the Renaissance Artists used the numeric of the Bible to condense ancient understanding.

In the center of the painting there are three open windows. In the perspective visual of the composition's depth, there is one large window centered behind Jesus, there is also one small window on the left of Jesus and another small window to the right of Jesus. These windows have multiple Biblical and scriptural messages; the windows of heaven.

The Last Supper…,
Da Vinci's Biblical Encoded Composition

The Biblical Codes of Da Vinci's Windows are **Metaphors of God's Numeric of Three:**

Wisdom Code Number 1:

The metaphor of the Cross of Calvary, The Lord is in the center, and the representation of the two other crosses of Calvary on the left and right of the Lord.

Scripture Reference…

John 19:18…Where they crucified him, and two other with him, on either side one, and Jesus in the midst.

To the right of the painting Da Vinci, added **_LIGHT_**; the repented thief on the cross of Calvary would represent the glory of this light. However, to the left of the painting, Da Vinci depicted the **_DARKNESS_**; the darkness of the non-believing thief.

Reference Scripture…

Matthew 27:38…Then were there two thieves crucified with him, one on the right hand, and another on the left.

Page 126
The Last Supper…,
Da Vinci's <u>Biblical</u> Encoded Composition

Wisdom Code Number 2:

The metaphor of the Seed of Woman, The Lord is the **<u>SEED</u>** of woman in the center of the large window; the smaller window to the left of the Lord depicts the Old Testament near the **<u>DARKENESS</u>** of the paneled walls; and the other smaller window to the right of the Lord, depicts the New Testament near the **<u>LIGHT</u>** of the paneled walls.

SPIRITUAL WAR; Heaven's War on Earth:

Da Vinci encoded the Bible's Spiritual War in the visual tenses; he encoded the past, the present, and the future by overlapping visual scriptural events.

$$(((((((((((+)))))))))))$$

The Last Supper is Da Vinci's visual culmination of God's curse and redemption mandate of Genesis 3:15 with the ancient symbol of "sacred feminine," womb of woman; the prophesied seed of the woman; the seed born of virgin.

Page 127
The Blood of Jesus…,
and the Blood of the Chalice???

<u>Where</u> is "The Last Supper's" Chalice?

The Wisdom of Da Vinci……Is the blood in the VIENS or is the blood in a CHALICE ?   Leonardo gave the painting the foresight of the physical present tense.

Most of the Renaissance Artist painted The Last Supper with a Chalice, the cup of Christ, but Leonardo da Vinci clearly kept within the logic of the moment in time, <u>the present</u>, because the blood of Jesus was still in his <u>veins</u>. Da Vinci knew that painting a chalice in the composition would conflict with the visual presence of a Jesus who was still alive. The blood of the chalice was still in the Savior's veins.

Da Vinci's, analytical reasoning in omitting the chalice in the Last Supper's painting would not have had any visual spiritual authority because Jesus was not yet crucified on the cross.

At the supper table, the Lord spoke in reference to the future tense; in remembrance of him. .

The Blood of Jesus…, and the Blood of the Chalice???

The very next day, the **future** would enter into GRACE and the BLOOD and WATER would be shed. The very next day, the Chalice would symbolically hold the Blood of Grace. Leonardo da Vinci had a mind-set of structured "Order."

The significance of the chalice for the blood, <u>is in the past tense;</u> the past tense of the next day. Even the essence of the scriptures refers to the past tense of……. REMEMBRANCE OF ME.

*Leonardo da Vinci chose not to paint the pending future of the CHALICE; the Blood to be; **<u>redemptive blood.</u>***

The Last Supper's composition shows the meal to be of fish and bread, not the traditional lamb, because he, Jesus, was the lamb to be slain; the Master Artist of the Renaissance Age knew all the spiritual angles and numeric of the Bible's sequences of authority. Da Vinci painted the condensed spiritual wisdom of the past and the present, hence, the glory of the future.

The Blood of Jesus…, and the Blood of the Chalice???

Furthermore, there are numerous panoramic glances that render the illusion of the **_Progressive Physics_** of the pre-existence; the pace of the present, of the past, and the pace of the future; progressive <u>time</u>.

Scripture Reference:

Luke 22:19…This is my body which is given for you: this do in remembrance of me.

1st Corinthians 11:25…After the same manner also he took the cup, when he had supped, saying, This cup is the new testament in my blood: this do ye, as oft as ye drink it, in remembrance of me.

In Da Vinci's Last Supper…, the Chalice or the Cup of Christ was not the inference of a Mary Magdalene, as the novel "The Da Vinci Code" has alleged. Leonardo da Vinci was very wise towards the Bible's sequential events, he had spiritual discernment of the dynamics of Biblical past, present, and future. Da Vinci knew that JESUS, himself, was the living Chalice.

What is the <u>Mystery</u> of Mary Magdalene?

<u>Mary Magdalene</u> was a woman in the crossroads of the Old Testament and the New Testament who was possessed by seven demons; she apparently was not under the subjection of **masculine** authority as most women were under-the-law; she was devoid of the masculine spiritual authority under the logistics of the Law.

<u>Mary Magdalene</u> was a woman who evidently did not have a rooted righteous family or the protection of God under-the-law; and evidently was in the clutches of spiritual war, tormented by demons. The Lord Jesus cast out her demons.

<u>Mary Magdalene</u> was a committed and devoted servant of The Lord and his disciples; the instance she gave her life to the Lord, she became part of the hedge of righteousness; a follower of the Christ; giver of eternal life. Magdalene also did not run in fear during and after the crucifixion; FEAR in essence is a **<u>sin</u>**.

Mary Magdalene…
The Innocent Truth

Mary Magdalene's enigma dwells in the factors of the seven demons, which possessed her soul. Her mystery is not complex when one considers and discerns the reason why demons would attack a person's soul in the first place. Magdalene's seven demons evidently originated from the demerits of a generational curse. She inherited a family curse; the curse enabled these demons to have authority over her. Under-the-law she apparently had no masculine guidance or immediate family. However, the Lord knew her **heart** and her spiritual calling.

Mary Magdalene…The Aramaic Connection; God is Covert

After 2000 years, the mystery factors of Mary Magdalene and her SEVEN demons still continue to perplex the world. This ancient mystery dwells in the significant factors of the earth's languages and Satan's proficiency of the languages and the knowledge thereof.

The core discernment of this mystery reverts to the omniscient powers of the **Mind of God** and with the ever-present aspects of the spiritual battle for the **mind of man;** the spiritual battle of evil is continuous within the principalities of the fallen earth.

Mary Magdalene…
The Innocent Truth

God is the sovereign navigator and originator of languages. During the Tower of Babel it was the "Logos" who confound the ONE language of men; this was when the whole earth was of one language, and of one speech.

But, when the Son of God came upon the earth, Jesus, he inherited and spoke a covert language **ORDERED** by heaven, but NOT KNOWN to Satan; this is the astounding ancient mystery of Aramaic. Satan has the acquired knowledge of what is spoken in *all* the languages of men, with the **exception of Aramaic.** The ancient language of Aramaic was the Mother Tongue of the Lord Jesus Christ; this was and is a sacred and divine language. All of Jesus followers also knew the language of Aramaic, "<u>including</u>" Mary Magdalene and the rest of the women in the Lord's circle. The Lord's language was Aramaic and he also prayed in Aramaic.

The ancient language of ARAMAIC is the only language on the earth that Satan and his demons **CANNOT DECIPHER** *or know the wisdom thereof.*

Here again, Satan knows all languages except for Aramaic. Satan is an entity that exists outside of the Logos, "**thought**," and Satan cannot read the **mind of man** unless…… a person is possessed by demons; **as was the woes of Mary Magdalene.**

Mary Magdalene…
The Innocent Truth

Mary Magdalene *knew* the language of Aramaic and because she was possessed by seven demons, this ancient language would have been cast into the Spiritual War, giving Satan the knowledge and authority of this sacred and exclusive language that was spoken by the Lord Jesus. This is the pivotal mystery factor of **Mary Magdalene** and the seven demons and the **Aramaic Connection**. Mary Magdalene was attacked by demons who possessed and tormented her soul and mind. The Lord Jesus, in his infinite ways, knew that Satan and his demons were also attempting to gain access to the sacred and divine wisdom of the language of The Lord of Lords and The King of Kings. Hence, by possessing Mary Magdalene's mind and soul, demons could have extracted the secrets and the knowledge of Aramaic. Near the sepulchre after Jesus arose from the dead, the Lord and Mary Magdalene spoke in Aramaic; this was a miraculous verbal encounter; John 20:16,17.

John 20:16,17…Jesus saith unto her, Mary. She turned herself, and saith unto him, Rabboni; which is to say, Master. Jesus saith unto her, Touch me not; for I am not yet ascended to my Father: but go to my brethren, and say unto them, I ascend unto my Father, and your Father; and to my God, and your God.

Mary Magdalene…
The Innocent Truth

The Factor of Speaking in Tongues:

Satan also **cannot** decipher the gift of speaking in tongues of the Holy Spirit. The gift of the **Baptism of the Holy Spirit** is a direct communicative line with the almighty Father.

Aramaic Data:

Syriac –Ancient Aramaic language spoken from the 3rd to the 13th century A.D., Eastern Mediterranean origin. During the Inter-Testamental period, Hebrew writing underwent great changes. The Jewish writers were strongly influenced by Aramaic on the Elephantine Island, Nile River.

Reference Scripture:
Towel of Babel

Genesis 11:6,7,8…And the LORD said, Behold, the people is one, and they have all one language; and this they begin to do: and now nothing will be restrained from them, which they have imagined to do. Go to, let us go down, and there confound their language, that they may not understand one another's speech. So the LORD scattered them abroad from thence upon the face of all the earth: and they left off to build the city.

Mary Magdalene...
The Innocent Truth

<u>Mary Magdalene</u>, has also been depicted by many of the Master Artists of the past, **with what is believed to be,** provocative sexual images with her beautiful hair, breast, face, and body of which, unfortunately, has cast the sexual perceptions of modern day innuendos. The Artistic truth of the composite is not of the sexual desires or appeal, but of the inheritance of the feminine beauty, the innocence of creation and of righteousness in the fabric of heaven on Earth.

In the Bible, for example, a woman hair is a form of her **glory** and a covering where angels camp around her; 1 Corinthians 11:15. Most of the history's Art masterpieces of Mary Magdalene are not, by any means, of sexual desires or fantasies; only the carnal mind reaps such negative thoughts.

The Hair
Reference Scripture:
1 Corinthisan 11:15…kjv

But if a woman have long hair, it is a glory to her: for her hair is given her for a covering.

Mary Magdalene…
The Innocent Truth

<u>Mary Magdalene</u> is the epitome of a feminine spiritual transition from demonic torment to the Lord's saving Grace. Before she approached Jesus of Nazareth she was spiritually and physically lost and tormented with seven demons, under-the-law. The Lord saw the suffering and repentance in her heart and gave her mercy and grace in the crossroads of Salvation.

The Gnostic mystics sought out a direct spiritual "line" of communications with God; bypassing the authoritative and universal **<u>provision</u>** *of the Lord Jesus; The Christ.*

The Gnostic gospel wrote about Mary Magdalene and Jesus deceivingly. The Gnostics were a crystal-ball type sect of heretical beliefs; they rebuked Jesus as the Lord and Savior; the Gnostics believed in a hocus-pocus direct telephone line with God, without the authority of the blood.

Jesus cured many infirmities, plagues, healed the deaf, gave sight to the blind, recovered the lame, and cast out evil spirits, but the wisdom of heaven is **<u>repentance</u>**.

What is the **Wisdom** of Repentance:

God..., the Ancient of Time, is a God of Love, God of laws, and also God of covenants and commandments. God desires us to be in oneness with him.

When mankind repents at 180 degrees, he dwells within the teachings, laws, and commandments of the Lord; grace and mercy;

*BUT, if mankind cunningly repents at 360 degrees, he has deceived himself and gives way to the **weaver's shuttle**, curses, chastisements, chastening, diseases, and death, because God, is Holy and his son taught three years of spiritual righteousness, conduct, and comportment, in **ADVANCE** of the purchase of sin. His son's divine blood which released us from underneath a form of Spiritual Marshall Law; God is a strict disciplinarian.*

Mary Magdalene…
The Innocent Truth

In the Old Testament there were seven (7) stages of the Feminine Factors:

1- There was the Feminine possessed, as was Mary Magdalene.

2- The Feminine of a Throne; as was Queen Esther.

3- The multitasked feminine of Prophetess, Judge, and Commander in God's Military Army; as that of Deborah; wife of Lapidoth.

4- The Feminine child, under-the-law, as in Mary the daughter of Lazarus.

5- The Feminine virgin maiden, as was Mary the Mother of Jesus.

6- The Feminine married woman, under-the-law, as in Elisabeth, wife of Zacharias and mother of John the Baptist.

7- The Feminine married, arrogant and disdainful, as that of Job's wife; under-the-law.

Mary Magdalene…
The Innocent Truth

Mary Magdalene was a devoted, humble servant of the Lord and of heaven's mandate. Historians portrayed her as the sinner who repented, a prostitute with demons. Critics and Historians will never find the perfect woman. Even under grace, there is nowhere to find the perfect and virtuous feminine in one single woman. The Bible has its share of evil women, but Mary Magdalene was a feminine soul who sought out Jesus in the crossroad before the blood was shed.

<u>*Virtuous Woman:*</u> *Where is a perfect woman to be found? King Solomon's heart dreamed and searched for the perfect virtuous woman.*

The Composite of the Virtuous Woman
Reference Scripture
Proverbs 31:10 –31…kjv

Who can find a virtuous woman? For her price is far above rubies. 11 The heart of her husband doth safely trust in her, so that he shall have no need of spoil. 12 She will do him good and not evil all the days of her life. 13 She seeketh wool, and flax, and worketh willingly with her hands. 14 She is like the merchants' ships; she bringeth her food from afar. 15 She riseth also while it is yet night, and giveth meat to

Page 140
Mary Magdalene…
The Innocent Truth

her household, and a portion to her maidens. 16 She considereth a field, and buyeth it: with fruit of her hands she planteth a vineyard. 17 She girdeth her loins with strength, and strengtheneth her arms. 18 She perceiveth that her merchandise is good: her candle goeth not out by night. 19 She layeth her hands to the spindle, and her hands hold the distaff. 20 She stretcheth out her hand to the poor; yea, she reacheth forth her hands to the needy. 21 She is not afraid of the snow for her household: for all her household are clothed with scarlet. 22 She maketh herself coverings of tapestry; her clothing is silk and purple. 23 Her husband is known in the gates, when he sitteth among the elders of the land. 24 She maketh fine linen, and selleth it; and delivereth girdles unto the merchant. 25 Strength and honour are her clothing; and she shall rejoice in time to come. 26 She openeth her mouth with wisdom; and in her tongue is the law of kindness. 27 She looketh well to the ways of her household, and eateth not the bread of idleness. 28 Her children arise up, and call her blessed; her husband also, and he praiseth her. 29 Many daughters have done virtuously, but thou excellest them all. 30 Favour is deceitful, and beauty is vain: but a woman that feareth the LORD, she shall be praised. 31 Give her of the fruit of her hands; and let her own works praise her in the gates.

Mary Magdalene…
The Innocent Truth

Mary Magdalene
Reference Scriptures:

Matthew 27:56…kjv
Among which was Mary Magdalene, and Mary the mother of James and Joses, and the mother of Zebedee's children.

Matthew 28:1…kjv
In the end of the Sabbath, as it began to dawn toward the first day of the week, came Mary Magdalene and the other Mary to see the sepulchre.

Matthew 28:5…kjv
And the angel answered and said unto the women, Fear not ye: for I know that ye seek Jesus, which was crucified.

Mark 16:9..kjv
Now when Jesus was risen early the first day of the week, he appeared first to Mary Magdalene, out of whom he had cast seven devils.

Luke 8:2..kjv
And certain women, which had been healed of evil spirits and infirmities, Mary called Magdalene, out of whom went seven devils,

Mary Magdalene…
The Innocent Truth

Luke 24:10…kjv
It was Mary Magdalene, and Joanna, and Mary the mother of James, and other women that were with them, which told these things unto the apostles.

John 19:25…kjv
Now there stood by the cross of Jesus his mother, and his mother's sister, Mary the wife of Cleophas, and Mary Magdalene.

John 20:1…kjv
The first day of the week cometh Mary Magdalene early, when it was yet dark, unto the sepulchre, and seeth the stone taken away from the sepulchre.

John 20:18…kjv
Mary Magdalene came and told the disciples that she had seen the Lord, and that he had spoken these things unto her.

Mary Magdalene…
The Innocent Truth

The <u>Hoax</u> of all Hoaxes,
……Bloodline of Magdalene & Jesus

How do you fed an ancient elephant to the population of the earth…a teaspoon everyday.

  …..a teaspoon of doubt per day

  …..a teaspoon of deception everyday

 AND by the time each person ingests the entire elephant, the mind of next pending generations will been re-programmed against God's gift of eternal life.

$$(((+)))$$

As the Evidence will reveal, Da Vinci's "The Last Supper" does **not** hide any codes of a sacred marriage or bloodline with Mary Magdalene and Jesus. Mary Magdalene was a sinner who became a servant of The LORD in the crucial crossroads of salvation. As the evidence will reveal, Mary Magdalene had a spiritual independence unlike any other repented feminine in prior history, Under-the-Law; status of.

SARAH ?...... Magdalene's daughter;
The Da Vinci Code Deception

The X <u>Chromosome</u> of Jesus

The **X** and **Y** DNA of the Earth?

In Dan Brown's novel "The Da Vinci Code" it is alleged that Jesus and Mary Magdalene started a bloodline within the French Royalty and that the name of their daughter was...... Sarah. It further plots evidence that Sarah's bloodline exist today.

*Romans 1:25…Who changed the truth of God into a lie, and worshipped and served the <u>**creature**</u> more than the <u>**Creator**</u>, who is blessed for ever. Amen.*

*Scientific Data: The Science of Divinity, Jesus **X** Chromosome?*

*In the genetic science of divinity, Jesus did not have an **X** Chromosome to render for procreation.*

SARAH ?...... Magdalene's daughter; The Da Vinci Code Deception

The scientific question is.... Did the genetics of Jesus have an **X** chromosome for the creation of a female child?......The alleged child of Mary Magdalene named Sarah.

Did the genetic <u>CODE</u> of the Lord Jesus possess an **X** chromosome for procreation of a feminine child? Jesus, was not begotten by **HUMAN SPERM**.

The specifics of chromosomes of the EARTH are as follows:

Scientifically, on the earth, the father's genetic code has an **X** and a **Y** chromosome. Also scientifically, on the EARTH, the sex of a child is determined by the father; the male only. The female's egg contains her own genetic code; both are fallen chromosomes.

The allegation that Jesus and Mary Magdalene had a child by the name of **SARAH**, dates back approximately nine hundred years and most recently with Dan Brown's Novel, "The Da Vinci Code;" it has further fueled this ancient deception, now analogized as a world-wide literary virus.

Page 146
SARAH ?...... Magdalene's daughter;
The Da Vinci Code, Deception

The Lord from heaven could **NOT** have inherited fallen chromosomes of mankind on the Earth because the Lord was 100% divine. Jesus did **NOT** inherit the genetic code of mankind's fallen DNA and chromosomes. The Lord was created by the quickening of the Holy Spirit in the womb of a virgin.

Jesus could not have started a bloodline with Mary Magdalene because his genetics did not inherit the scientific physiology of the origin of sin. The Lord Jesus did not genetically possess an **X** chromosome because he was **NOT** procreated from the **SPERM OF MAN**; the fallen chromosomes of mankind's seed. On the earth the sperm of mankind is fallen and flawed.

Jesus was the Second Adam. In the Garden of Eden, the first Adam was ***ready pigmented*** with heaven's mandate of divine chromosomes; before sin, Adam never inherited any DNA for the Animal Kingdom.

SARAH ?...... Magdalene's daughter; The Da Vinci Code, Deception

Eve, was made from the pre-existing divine genetics of Adam. But......., after Adam and Eve sinned all of mankind's genetics fell; then diseases infiltrated the body and the human genetics. After sin came into the world, four governing factors followed consequence in the spiritual realm and in the scientific world. These factors that ensued are as follows…the fallen soul, man's fallen seed of birth, the animal kingdom fell, and the **EARTH** fell. The human chromosomes became flawed, defective and imperfect after evil entered the world. Before sin man was able to communicate with the animals and his environment.

In Genesis 3:17,18, 19, God cursed the **MAN**, God cursed the **WOMAN**, God cursed the **SERPENT**, and spoke that the **EARTH** was also cursed because of their disobedience.

Jesus could not have started a bloodline with Mary Magdalene because his scientific genetics code did not possess an **X** chromosome.

SARAH ?…… Magdalene's daughter;
The Da Vinci Code, Deception

The discerning truth of the Bible is INFALLIBLE. Jesus was the **Second Adam** with divine chromosomes; mankind has fallen chromosomes. Jesus was the Lord from heaven in the flesh of divinity. The Lord was made a quickening Spirit into the womb of a virgin. The Virgin Mary…….Luke 1:42 "blessed is the fruit of they womb." The Virgin Mary's genetics were ordered by God and guarded within the generations from Abraham down to the lineage Joseph her husband to be.

In the book of Hebrews, Chapter Four, God hast prepared the Lord a body, for the Lord came to do the will of God.

Hebrews 10:4,5…For it is not possible that the blood of bulls and of goats should take away sins. 5 Wherefore when he cometh into the world, he saith, Sacrifice and offering thou wouldest not, but a body hast thou prepared me:

1st Corinthians 15:45,46,47
And so it is written, The first man Adam was made a living soul: the last Adam was made a quickening spirit. 46 Howbeit that was not first which is spiritual, but that which is natural; and afterward that which is spiritual. 47 The first man is of the earth, earthy: the second man is the Lord from heaven.

Page 149
SARAH ?...... Magdalene's daughter;
The Da Vinci Code, Deception

Scripture Reference:

John 1:1,2

In the beginning was the Word, and the Word was with God, and the Word was God. 2 The same was in the beginning with God.

John 1:14

And the word was made flesh, and dwelt among us, (and we beheld his glory as of the only begotten of the Father,) full of grace and truth.

Jesus was 100% divine in the flesh and 100% divine in his soul. The Lord Jesus chromosomes were of the Masculine ORDER of heaven. **God** *is Masculine,* **Jesus** *is Masculine, and the* **Holy Spirit** *is Masculine. The trinity of the Godhead is Masculine.* **Adam,** *was masculine, formed by the Masculine Order of God.*

SARAH ?…… Magdalene's daughter;
The Da Vinci Code, Deception

Before sin, Adams chromosomes were pure and divine from the earth. Jesus chromosomes were not of the fallen earth. Jesus could not have started a bloodline with Mary Magdalene because his genetics did not possess an **X** chromosome. They could not have spawned a Holy Bloodline because Satan would have **WON**…… the equation of eternal authority.

In order to understand the science of the feminine physics, it must be traced back to the origin of the X chromosome, before and after sin in Genesis.

Before the human female physically appeared on the earth, everything on the earth was already created and firmly established by God. Before the female was made by God, manifested in the Rhema, everything on the earth was foundationally established; all of nature was in complete harmony with God.

Page 151
SARAH ?...... Magdalene's daughter;
The Da Vinci Code, Deception

The waters brought forth the moving **creature**, and the fowl that may fly above the earth in the open, and God created great whales, and every living **creature** that moveth after their kind, and every winged fowl after his kind, and God said let the earth bring forth the living **creature** after his kind, cattle, and creeping thing, and beast of the earth after his kind, and every herb bearing seed was upon the face of the earth, and every tree yielding seed.

All of the birds, the fish, the cattle, the animal kingdom, the plants, the herbs, and Adam were in harmony with God. Everything, everything was created before God made the feminine; the female was the last **manifestation** of the spoken word of creation.

Before God made the female, everything on the earth also, had its own genetic code of instructions. All of God's creations had their own biological physics and genetic code and DNA.

The female in essence was with the logos, "*__thought__,*" then made from the substance of the masculine. The female was made, not formed, but Adam, the masculine, was created in the radiance of the day; in the glory of the day.

Page 152
SARAH ?...... Magdalene's daughter;
The Da Vinci Code, Deception

The man was formed out of the dust of the ground; Genesis 2:17. The woman was made from the man, Genesis 2:22. The female was taken from the pre-existing genetics of the male. The female's genetics came from the male's bone; the masculine bone and marrow; in the Hebrew is it called the curve.

Scientifically, all new blood is always being made inside our bones. The woman was made from the bone genetics of a man; all new blood originates within the bones.

The **X** chromosome is the physics of the fallen genetics of mankind. The physics of the **X** chromosome is the biology of pre-existing genetics **AFTER** the spiritual offense of **SIN**; hence, genetic breakdown. God is the sovereign creator of all sciences, omnipresent. The **X** chromosome did not have human existence before Eve was made; bone of the masculine bone, propagated by God. The origin of the **X** chromosome dates back to God's curse in Genesis 3:17; the curse of genetics.

...For the man was not made of woman, but the woman of the man

Page 153
SARAH ?...... Magdalene's daughter;
The Da Vinci Code, Deception

Genesis 2:21, 22...And the LORD God caused a deep sleep to fall upon Adam, and he slept: and he took one of his ribs, and closed up the flesh instead thereof; 22 And the rib which the LORD God had taken from man, made he a woman, and brought her unto the man.

*Let us go back to Genesis when the earth was cursed per the **choice** of Adams and Eve's disobedience.*

Genesis 3:17...And unto Adam he said, Because thou hast hearkened unto the voice of thy wife, and hast eaten of the tree, of which I commanded thee, saying, Thou shalt not eat of it: cursed is the ground for thy sake; in sorrow shalt thou eat of it all the days of thy life;

18 Thorns also and thistles shall it bring forth to thee; and thou shalt eat the herb of the field: 19 In the Sweat of thy face shalt thou eat bread, till thou return unto the ground; for out of it wast thou taken: for dust thou art, and unto dust shalt thou return.

SARAH ?...... Magdalene's daughter;
The Da Vinci Code, Deception

*The genetics of Jesus could not have had a bloodline on the earth **scientifically**.*

In the Old Testament the last time a form of divinity took wives and bore children was in Genesis 6:1. Here we have the authority of the Sons of God giving children to the daughters of men.

*Genesis 6:1...And it came to pass, when men began to multiply on the face of the earth, and daughters were born unto them, 2 That the **sons of God** saw the daughters of men that they were fair, and they took them wives of all which they chose.*

Now, these were daughters of the genetics of men, the genetics of the X and Y Chromosomes. Of course, the sequence of the Bibles establishes that these were daughters of men after the fall of Adam and Eve.

SARAH ?...... Magdalene's daughter; The Da Vinci Code, Deception

The **Sons of God** in the Old Testament were Angels, but the **Sons of God** in the New Testament refer to mankind, the saints "In-Christ." The reason being, that after Adam sinned, God's angels immediately gained authority over man. Immediately after Adam and Eve sinned, a Cherubim took control of the Garden with a flaming sword, inheriting authority; the angels instantly took possession of the **Garden** when Adam and Eve were cast out.

The Angels were **created** by God. Adam was **made** by God; but Eve was **formed** by God, all three have separate dimensions of origin existence. The Lord Jesus was made lower than the Angels, because the earth was **under-the-law**; spiritual war.

*Hebrew 2:8...But we see Jesus, who was made a **little lower than the angels** for the suffering of death, crowned with glory and honour; that he by the grace of God should taste death for every man.*

Psalms 8:4,5.......What is man, that thou art mindful of him? And the son of man, that thou visitest him? For thou has made him a little lower than the angels, and hast crowned him with glory and honour.

Page 156
SARAH ?...... Magdalene's daughter;
The Da Vinci Code, Deception

These daughters of men of fallen chromosomes produced an offspring of giants. Now, the Bible refers to giants to be approximately 9 ½ feet tall (Six cubits and a span) yet some scholars believe the giants to be 13 (thirteen) feet tall.

*Genesis 6:4.. There were giants in the earth in those days; and also after that, when the **sons of God** came in unto the daughters of men, and they bare children to them, the same became mighty men which were of old, men of renown.*

The mystery factors of Genesis 6:2, that of the **Sons of God**, the Bible refers to them as fallen angels. All forms of divinity do not have an **X** chromosome. Now, heavenly **angels are asexual**, however, these angels are **fallen** divinity on the EARTH; called the Sons of God.

These supernatural encounters took the daughters of men which produced more giants in the land......,but subsequently and consequently God destroyed all these offspring giants in the Flood of Noah. The **X** chromosome does not exist in the divine ORDER OF HEAVEN; the **Feminine X** and the other chromosomes of mankind, came from the CURSE in the Garden; genetics thereof, hence, physics thereof.

Page 157
SARAH ?...... Magdalene's daughter; The Da Vinci Code, Deception

In the Bible, we also know that these Sons of God were of spiritual authority, because in the Book of Job it also makes reference to these angels that approached the Lord….and Satan was in the same realm; same spiritual entourage, *so to speak*.

Job 1:6...Now there was a day when the sons of God came to present themselves before the Lord, and Satan came also among them. And the Lord said unto Satan, Whence comest thou? Then Satan answered the Lord, and said, from going to and fro in the earth, and from walking up and down in it.

There again, these giants of Genesis 6:2 is the only reference of the supernatural from the origin of heaven, bearing children with the daughters of men on the fallen earth. But as the Bible declares Noah's flood destroyed them.

*Here again, Jesus could not have started a bloodline with Mary Magdalene because his divine genetics did not possess an X chromosome; the Holy Spirit took **authority** of the virgin's DNA.*

SARAH ?...... Magdalene's daughter;
The Da Vinci Code, Deception

The scriptures declare, that God prepared a body for The Lord for salvation…. never for a marriage.

Jesus could not become (**One Flesh**) in marriage with Mary Magdalene who was born with the genetics of the sin origin herself and her alleged daughter who was named Sarah could not have ever existed because Jesus did not possess a fallen X chromosome; hence, the **genetics of sperm**; chromosomes.

To further trace the X chromosome back to Genesis, we must remember that the genetics of the bone and bone marrow of Adam was given to Eve when God made her. In essence, Adam's bone substance was propagated for the female, which God cursed after sin entered the garden. The X chromosome equates to the physics of the fallen Eve and God's unfolding curse on the feminine factors on the earth, which has been traced through the Human DNA and the Mitochondrial DNA. In Creation Science, the Mitochondrial DNA differs with modern science only in the Biblical theology of years; time span.

SARAH ?...... Magdalene's daughter; The Da Vinci Code, Deception

Biblically, human genetics are from the direct fallout of sin; God's curse. The feminine, Eve, was made from the genetics of the Masculine bone; Eve, was also made during the **PHYSICS OF SLEEP**. This is why in the theory of Biblical Science the **feminine** is inherently and genetically capable of restoring lost sleep, **but the masculine cannot** restore his lost sleep or sleep deprivation. This is the vital underlining mystery of the longevity factors of the females over the males; the creation science of sleep, <u>Adam was of the physics of the day</u>. The physics of the feminine has the capacity of recovering lost sleep because she was made from the substance of Adam's pre-existing genetics. The Biblical root of the creation physics of the X chromosome is directly correlated to the origin of the Feminine X.

Genesis 2:21…kjv
And the LORD God caused a deep sleep to fall upon Adam, and he slept: and he took one of his ribs, and closed up the flesh instead thereof;

Genesis 3:16…Unto the woman he said, I will greatly multiply thy sorrow and they conception; in sorrow thou shalt bring forth children; and thy desire shall be to thy husband, and he shall rule over thee.

*Jesus did not inherit an X chromosome to render unto the genetics of an earthly bloodline because his chromosomes are not of the origin of **cursed sperm**.*

Page 160
SARAH ?...... Magdalene's daughter;
The Da Vinci Code, Deception

The genetics of Jesus did not inherit an **X** chromosome for the creation of a female child; the **INFANT** Jesus was not procreated from the fallen seed of a man. Jesus, did **NOT** inherit the fallen **X** chromosome from the Holy Spirit. The Holy Spirit was **NOT** of human sperm. The Lord Jesus was from **Heaven's Masculine Order.**

The Fallen Human Genetics Within the Scientific Data:

Science today has confirmed all the essential properties that constitute our Human DNA. Our Human DNA has four different elements.

Scientifically, we share 98% of our DNA with chimpanzees, fallen DNA from the animal kingdom. We also share a small percentage (1/2%) of our DNA with fruit flies, the fallen kingdom of insects. Scientifically, we share our DNA with (3/4%) of dogs; and a tiny percent of our human DNA with a botanical.

Page 161
SARAH ?...... Magdalene's daughter;
The Da Vinci Code, Deception

The fallen human genetics are the direct links of the fallen earth after sin; **mankind's separation from God,** his creator. It is interesting to note, that the above data on the science of Human DNA has equations of curses in the Bible. In the Bible there are THIRTY-ONE BOOKS referencing the curses and factors of dogs. Also in the Bible, Matthew 23:24 it refers to the Fruit Fly. The Bible calls the Fruit Fly a **GNAT**; the Gnat is the origin species of the fruit fly and the mosquito. The Gnat is also called poison in the Greek.

Now, why would God prepare a body for the Lord with the shared genetics of dogs and fruit flies, the factors of curses and infestations rejected in the Bible.

Jesus DNA and chromosomes were divine. Again, the Bible declares that God prepared a body for the Lord. God would never prepare a body for his son with fallen chromosomes of dogs, chimpanzees, and fruit flies.

Adam and Eve were not created through a birth canal. Jesus was the Second Adam.

Page 162
SARAH ?...... Magdalene's daughter;
The Da Vinci Code, Deception

Scientifically, the **Y** and **X** chromosomes only exist in the genetics of the cursed and fallen earth; humanity's DNA and chromosomes are flawed and damaged. Also, the **Y** chromosome and its mutations, properties thereof, are of the Genesis 3:17.18.19 curse. The Lord Jesus did not come to recover the fallen earth or to bring peace; Christ, the Savior, came to redeem the **SOUL.**

Matthew 10:34…Think not that I am come to send peace on earth: I came not to send peace, but a sword.

Cleansing a Lineage for the Holy Spirit

Matthew 1:17
So all the generations from Abraham to David are fourteen generations; and from David until the carrying away into Babylon are fourteen generations; and from the carrying away into Babylon unto Christ are fourteen generations.

Was it Blood for Salvation…. or
Blood for Procreation?

*Was the Blood of Jesus mandated by God for **Salvation** or for a bloodline in a **marriage**…; hence the Mary Magdalene deception.*

The Biblical **Blood** & Lineage Of Jesus…

*God divinely guided thousands of years to cleanse and make perfect "The Bloodline of Jesus." God **prepared** a body…for the Lord.*

The Lineage of Jesus:

Matthew 1:1 – 16…..kjv
The book of generation of Jesus Christ, the son of David, the son of Abraham. 2 Abraham begat Issac; and Issac begat Jacob; and Jacob begat Judas and his brethren; 3 And Judas begat Phares and zara of Thamar; and Phares begat Esrom; and Esrom begat Aramm; 4 And Aram begat Aminadab; and Aminadab begat Naasson; and Naasson begat Salmon; 5 And Salmon begat Booz of Rachab; and Booz begat Obed of Ruth; and Obed begat Jesse; 6 And Jesse begat David the king; and

Was it Blood for Salvation…. or Blood for Procreation?

God Prepared a body…The Lineage of Jesus continued:

David the King begat Solomon of her that had been the wife of Urias; 7 And Solomon begat roboam; and Roboam begat Abia; and Abia begat Asa; 8 And Asa begat Josaphat; and Josephat begat Joram; and Joram begat Ozias; 9 And Ozias begat Joatham; and Joatham begat Achaz; and Achaz begat Ezekias; 10 And Ezekias begat Menasseh; and Manasseh begat Amon; and Amon begat Josias; 11 And Josias begat Jechonias and his brethren, about the time they were carried away to Babylon: 12 And after they were brought to Babylon, jechonias begat Salathiel; and salathiel begat Zoroabel; 13 And Zorobabel begat Abiud; and Abiud begat Eliakim; and Eliakim begat Azor; 14 And Azor begat Sadoc; and Sadoc begat Achim; and Achim begat Eliud; 15 And Eliud begat Eleazar; and Eleazar begat Matthan; and Matthan begat Jacob; 16 And Jacob begat Joseph the husband of Mary, of whom was born Jesus, <u>who is called Christ.</u>

Was it Blood for Salvation.... or Blood for Procreation?

Discern…!

Jesus and Mary Magdalene; Blood for a Marriage **Cancels** the Blood of Salvation

Biblical Discernment:

The core deception is the claim that Jesus and Mary Magdalene were married and that they produced a bloodline that exist today. In the Word of God, the Blood of Jesus could not have been compromised for the world's genetics, the pool of DNA of the earth.

*A marriage of Jesus on the earth, would have **CANCELLED ALL** of the redemptive powers for Salvation.*

*Jesus came to the fallen earth, as the savior for mankind's sins; **NOT** to procreate a bloodline that he himself would judge on Judgment Day.*

Was it Blood for Salvation…. or Blood for Procreation?

If Jesus and Mary Magdalene had been married, the marriage and her pregnancy would have totally cancelled, *annihilated*, the redemptive powers of the **BLOOD** on the cross. The **BLOOD** on the cross was secured by heaven for one purpose only, the purchase of sin; the redemption of man.

The discernment of the Bible is irrefutable, for Jesus to have started a bloodline on the earth, this would have totally destroyed and annihilated all hopes for the salvation of mankind, because the **BLOOD** of the Savior could never, never, be contaminated in the earth's genetics. The **BLOOD** of the Savoir could have never been predisposed in the Womb of Woman; especially in a womb of a woman made by the sperm, (*seed*), of man.

The **BLOOD** of Christ was not cleansed for forty-two generation in order to leave it behind in the lineages of the fallen earth. The Blood of Christ could not have been left behind in a womb of a woman. The **BLOOD** of Christ was for Salvation's sacrifice in its totality.

Was it Blood for Salvation…. or
Blood for Procreation?

For Jesus to have married Mary Magdalene, his blood would have been cast aside and detoured into the Spiritual War of the fallen earth.

What is the __Biblical Evidence__ that Jesus was not married?

The evidence is in the <u>Dominion Factor</u>.
The evidence is in the <u>Factors of Judgment Day</u>, and throughout the equations of the scriptures.

The **BLOOD** of Christ was not protected for forty-two generations in order to leave it behind in the lineages of the fallen earth; the **BLOOD** was not <u>in vain</u>. The **BLOOD** of Christ was for salvation, a sacrifice of love in its totality.

The Blood of Jesus could have never compromised for the world's genetics.

Was it Blood for Salvation…. or Blood for Procreation?

*The **Heresy** of all Heresies Within the Sinister Christian Church*

The Holy Grail legend of a marriage between Jesus and Mary Magdalene is a nine hundred year deception. This veracious paranoia was of the origin of the confounded minds of the sinister fabric of the church of that era. The **forked mind** of that era did not bathe in Biblical discernments, but only in the destructive parallels of GREED, POWER, and SPIRITUAL PARANOIA. This nine hundred year old deception, traveled through the corridors of the sinister Church, Europe, and into the royal thrones of dysfunctional, sexually insane, and inbreeding rulers.

This deceit and false theory was like the tentacles of an octopus, maintaining a strangling grip against Biblical truths and discernment. Dan Brown's novel "The Da Vinci Code." further amplified the deception, embellishing the malignance of these "so-called" secrets throughout the world.

Was it Blood for Salvation…. or Blood for Procreation?

The novel introduced doubt to Christianity's core. The strangling tentacles or the poisonous roots of the Holy Grail story of a marriage between Jesus and Mary Magdalene does not have any Biblical foundation whatsoever. These ancient secrets were fermented within the dark sinister authorities of the Catholic Church of that era.

The scriptures declare that God himself confounds the mind of man; God is the logos, **Elohim,** he can and will confound the mind of man while he laughs in the heavens at the deceiver. The origin of our languages today are of God's direct curse of the confound mind to the populous of the **Tower of Babel.**

It was also stated that Jesus was a Jewish man and that by Jewish law, at his age, he would be married. We must remember that Jesus was the Lord, quickened by the Holy Spirit in a virgin womb. Jesus was the Lord born within a Jewish bloodline, a chosen race. When Jesus reappeared at the age of thirty (30) he was beyond the recommend Jewish age; Jesus was the second Adam and the Lord of Lords.

Was it Blood for Salvation.... or Blood for Procreation?

The earthly age of **Jesus the Christ,** is the constituent of the direct numerical equations of heaven's cosmos and the Plan of Salvation for the Earth.

For Example:

The spiritual numerical equation of the Lord Jesus is **33.** (thirty-three)… plus…decimal… 3 (three). ($33.333333333…$ equals…1st Heaven).

The spiritual numerical equation of God **WITHOUT the Authority** of Jesus is **66.** (sixty-six)… plus…decimal…6 (six). (2nd Heaven $= 33.333333333$)   (3rd Heaven$=33.333333333$)

The numerical equation of the Authority of the Lord Jesus **WITH the FATHER GOD** is **99.**999999999.

Leonardo Da Vinci comprehended all the spiritual mathematical equations of earth and heaven, as his spiritual paintings and sketches reveal.

Was it Blood for Salvation…. or Blood for Procreation?

God would have **never** sent his son to propagate the **BLOOD** of salvation prior to the cross. The **BLOOD** on the cross was secured by God for one purpose only, to redeem mankind; the purchase of sin. The **BLOOD** of Jesus could not be compromised for the genetics of mankind; human genetics came from the **CURSE**; origin of sin.

Mankind is only righteous through the redemptive **BLOOD**. The redemptive **BLOOD** could never be left behind in the veins of descendants; lineages of the fallen world, because a bloodline of Jesus would be subject to judgment at the end of time by the Lord himself. The **BLOOD** of the Savior could have never been predisposed in the womb of woman. The **BLOOD** of Christ could not have a dual purpose. For the **BLOOD** to service as a double purpose for a **marriage and salvation** it would have voided the directives of God's Salvation of the Human Soul.

For the **BLOOD** of Jesus to have taken a detoured into human veins, prior to crucifixion, would have literally damned all souls on the earth.

Was it Blood for Salvation…. or Blood for Procreation?

Mary Magdalene was just another Saint of the Church; Jesus is the future husband of the Church; the Church is the Lord's Bride. For Jesus to have been married to Mary Magdalene, his **BLOOD** would have been cast aside and plunged into an eternal wasteland; hence, victory for Satan.

The *Evidence* of the Dominion Factor:

God gave dominion unto human procreation; the Lord God did not give dominion unto himself in Genesis.

Genesis 1:26…And God said, Let us make man in our image, after our likeness: and let them have dominion over the fish of the sea, and over the fowl of the air, and over the cattle, and over all the earth, and over every creeping thing that creepeth upon the earth.

Genesis 1:28…And God blessed them, and God said unto them, Be fruitful, and multiply, and replenish the earth, and subdue it: and have dominion over the fish of the sea, and over the fowl of the air, and over every living thing that moveth upon the earth.

Was it Blood for Salvation…. or Blood for Procreation?

*The life of mankind is in the **BLOOD**; after sin entered the world with Adam and Eve's disobedience, the redemption of mankind is in the **BLOOD of Christ.***

The trinity of the Godhead gave dominion unto mankind, NOT unto himself. Now for Jesus to have a bloodline on the earth, this would take away mankind's rights of dominion, because in Genesis 1:26 it reads "God said, Let them have dominion **OVER ALL THE EARTH**. God never said, let them have partial dominion until the son of God procreates a bloodline unto himself.

In 1st Corinthians 15:45, 47……..gives further evidence that Jesus was 100% divine in spirit and 100% divine in the flesh.

In 1st Corinthians 15:45,47
And so it is written, The first man Adam was made a living soul: the last Adam was made a quickening spirit. 47 The first man is of the earth, earthy: the second man is the Lord from heaven.

Page 174
Was it Blood for Salvation…. or
Blood for Procreation?

Summary:

1- *Jesus flesh was as the Second Adam.*

2- *Jesus was made by the quickening of the Holy Spirit.*

3- *Jesus was the Lord from heaven*

In Genesis 1:26, who said "**LET THEM HAVE DOMINION**," it was the divinity of the Father, the Son, and the Holy Spirit; so who also said "let them have dominion;" the Lord himself said "Let them have dominion." When God spoke, "LET US," give them dominion, the Lord was **WITH** God, the Lord is 1/3 of the trinity of God.

The Blood of Jesus could never be compromised for the fallen world's genetics and the contamination pool of DNA. The earth is the dominion of mankind, not the Savior.

*Jesus could not procreate a bloodline unto himself, because he gave the **dominion authority** to the Man.*

Was it Blood for Salvation…. or Blood for Procreation?

God could not have given the Man authority and dominion of over all the earth in order to cancel the dominion for a bloodline with Mary Magdalene; a bloodline with Mary Magdalene would rescind and cancel the spoken word within the Trinity of God of Genesis 1:26 and Genesis 1:28.

*The Bible states that we must discern and rightfully divide the word of God; the **BLOOD** of Jesus was the purchased price.*

Before the Crucifixion the BLOOD of Salvation could have not taken a detour and entered into the genetics of humanity. The Core of Christianity is the BLOOD that was shed completely without the contamination of a bloodline in the genetics of the earth. The Blood of Jesus could not have been left behind in the veins of genetics. The BLOOD of Jesus could not have been left behind in the womb of woman; a woman made from the seed of man.

Was it Blood for Salvation…. or Blood for Procreation?

The dominion of the earth was spoken, "Let **US** make man"… meaning that the Lord, and the Holy Spirit was **with God** and he commanded procreation to his people, this was not a future command for the Lord to Procreate himself into the Genesis equation.

Genesis 1:22…kjv
And God blessed them, saying, Be fruitful, and multiply, and fill the waters in the seas, and let fowl multiply in the earth.

Genesis: 1:26…kjv
And God said, Let us make man in our image, after our likeness: and let them have dominion over the fish of the sea, and over the fowl of the air, and over the cattle, and over all the earth, and over every creeping thing that creepeth upon the earth.

In Genesis 1:22…the Lord gave to the man and woman, a one-way command, not a command to spiritually **Retro-activate himself** into "woman," the human equations or into the bloodlines of royals, within the fallen earth.

Was it Blood for Salvation…. or Blood for Procreation?

The Lord is the Royal of all Royals, Lord of Lords, and King of Kings…,

*………and his blood was mandated for Salvation explicitly. The LORD himself could have **never** started a bloodline that he himself would have to Judge at the end of time.*

*At the **White Throne of Judgment**, the Lord, himself, would be the sovereign authority to judge and possibly destroy and send to hell his own lineage.*

*In essence, Dan Brown's allegations of a bloodline of Jesus and Mary Magdalene, would have in fact, **cancelled** the salvation of all humanity. God looks at our sins through the BLOOD of Jesus, shed in its totality, never through any **PRE-CRUCIFIXION** blood complexities of **Genetics**.*

*God did not want any more **borrowed** blood from the Animal Kingdom; hence, he prepared a body for The Lord.*

Was it Blood for Salvation…. or Blood for Procreation?

Reference Scriptures

Matthew 10:34,35…kjv

Think not that I am come to send peace on earth: I came not to send peace, but a sword. 35 For I am come to set a man at variance against his father, and the daughter against her mother, and the daughter in law against her mother in law.

Luke 4:18, 19…kjv

The Spirit of the Lord is upon me, because h e hath anointed me to preach the gospel to the poor; he hath sent me to heal the brokenhearted, to preach deliverance to the captives, and recovering of sight to the blind, to set a liberty them that are bruised, 19 To preach the acceptable year of the Lord.

((((((Blood of Man))))))

))))))))))Blood of Christ((((((((((

Da Vinci and God…;
The Wisdom of Darkness

Da Vinci's Wisdom of Shade and Light…; *thence Darkness*

Did Leonardo da Vinci comprehend the creation phases of the Science of Darkness?

The answer to this question…, we may never know definitively, however, based on his encoded Biblical and spiritual paintings the **Wisdom of Darkness** is very Biblically evident. Da Vinci sketched various intriguing studies of the **interception of light.** Some of Leonardo's spiritual compositions also manifest the pre-existence of darkness.

The following are some of Da Vinci's quotes on shade and darkness.

Da Vinci Quote:
"Shade has more power than light,…light can never completely displace shade, at least not that of solid bodies."

Da Vinci and God...;
The Wisdom of Darkness

Da Vinci Quote:

"Shade is of infinite darkness and there is an infinite number of gradations when moving from darkness to light...Shade is the means of revealing the shape of bodies."

Discernment:

Life and all **origins** of life were created and born within the fabric of the created **DARKNESS**.

Everything..., Everything such as light, planets, moons, stars, quasars, comets, galaxies, black-holes, cosmic volcanoes, ice, gases, chemicals, etcetera, etcetera, were formed and created within DARKNESS. The Lord creates DARKNESS where the light dwells in infinite existence; DARKNESS has a physical authority in the universe. Isaiah 45:7...I form the light, and create darkness:

Da Vinci and God…;
The Wisdom of Darkness

In creation, Darkness does not physically move, but Darkness does stretch and expand within itself. In the physical universe, DARKNESS expands and by expanding it advances. However, light was created on the fabric and grid of DARKNESS where it moves and travels. Light, also houses itself within the pool table of DARKNESS.

In our modern world of technology and medicine we can now spiritually calculate, that mankind needs 66.6% (percent) of light per day and 33.3% of darkness… per the twenty-four (24) hour day.

DARKNESS…has Spiritual and Physical properties

Darkness reference scriptures
Genesis 1:2…kjv
And the earth was without form, and void; and darkness was upon the face of the deep. And the Spirit of God moved upon the face of the waters.

Da Vinci and God…;
The Wisdom of Darkness

Isaiah 45:7…kjv
I form the light, and create darkness: I make peace, and create evil: I the LORD do all these things.

Ecclesiastes 11:8…kjv
But if a man live many years, and rejoice in them all; yet let him remember the days of darkness; for they shall be many. All that cometh is vanity.

Psalm 105:28…kjv
He sent darkness, and made it dark; and they rebelled not against his word.

Psalm 143:1…kjv
Behold, bless ye the LORD, all ye servants of the LORD, which by night stand in the house of the LORD.

Psalm 136:7,8,9…kjv
To him that made great lights: for his mercy endureth for ever: 8 The sun to rule by day: for his mercy endureth for ever: 9 The moon and stars to rule by night: for his mercy endureth for ever.

The Gnostics Rejected Jesus…; hence,
the Canon of God Reject the Gnostics.

Whence, Cometh Gnostic Authority……?
Devoid of Oaths and Vows

INTRO:

The Gnostic gospels do not have divine authority or credibility. Gnostics were also mystics, and their fundamental nature was the equivalency of psychics with nuances of witchcraft; their spiritual liberties of the mind dwelled in emulations and mysticism; these heretical beliefs of the Gnostics were the key factors that disqualified them from the canonization of the Holy Bible.

2nd Chronicles 33:6…And he caused his children to pass through the fire in the valley of the son of Hinnom: also he observed times, and used enchantments, and used witchcraft, and dealt with a familiar spirit, and with wizards: he wrought much evil in the sight of the LORD, to provoke him to anger.

God dwells and manifests his "Will" and truth through the Holy Spirit, covenants, and in powers of **oaths** and **vows**; and God inspires the mind through the anointed powers of his chosen.

Gnostics Rejected Jesus…; hence,
the Canon of God Reject the Gnostics.

God is a God of structured "Order" and perfection; God renders authoritative powers, **in forum,** to churches, to holy men and to Christianity's Royal Thrones of Kings and Queens. God's "**Will**" is manifested in the confides of "Solemn Order," oaths and vows received within the third (3rd) heaven. These authorities and powers are given to holy men appointed by God, in the first Jerusalem.

The Gnostics, *mystically* wanted a direct relationship with God, but not with Jesus, and without the authority and the name of God's son, the Gnostics, in reality, became a renegade religious sect.

God does not authorize powers to any Christian outcasts of grievances or factions with thwarted intent. God will never bless discontented, non-oath, non-vowed, heretical believers who invent God's **"WILL."**

The Holy Bible was canonized under the authority of the Holy Spirit and with irrevocable oaths held in heaven.

Hence…….; whence, cometh Gnostic authority?
    *From the quagmire of **Satan's authorship**.*

Jesus and Mary Magdalene, A <u>Holy</u> Kiss or A Gnostic Kiss?

The Bible's <u>Holy</u> Kiss

In the <u>non-authorized</u> Gnostic gospels, the Book of Philip has a passage which reads that Jesus kissed Mary Magdalene often and that his disciples were jealous of their relationship. Dan Brown's novel infers that this is more evidence that Jesus and Mary Magdalene were married and that they started a bloodline within the French Royalty.

The mere fact that Jesus might have kissed Mary Magdalene does not render evidence that they were married. The discerning Biblical truth is that if Jesus had transferred his blood genetically before the Salvation factors of humanity, the act of the marriage and procreation of a child would have **cancelled the Salvation** of all of mankind on the earth. The discerning truth of scriptures are that God did not orchestrate forty-two generations to cleanse the blood for our salvation only to cancel its redeeming powers in a pre-crucifixion marriage.

Page 186
The Holy Kiss;
Jesus and Mary Magdalene

Jesus was the Lord God, his love for Mary Magdalene was that of the Agape love. Agape love is a love that is willing to die for another.

Based on the fixed divine "ORDER" of God, the Gnostic gospels were not authorized by God, the Gnostics were not men led by the Holy Spirit; they were mystics that rejected the authority of Jesus as the Son of God.

The Gnostics were authors of spiritual confusion; hence, their cosmic *thoughts and hocus pocus* rendered the devil in the details. The "love" that the Gnostics profess for God does not exist in the realm of heaven. Gnostic "love" **only** exists in the realm of pride and in the realm of exalting oneself. The Biblical God of the universe has only four loves which mankind directly **inherits.** These four loves were taught by and through Christ Jesus; they are Agape love, Phileo Love, Storge Love, and Eros Love. All other loves belong to the spiritual darkness which exists only in the spirit of **Satan.** In addition to being a deceiver of the **mind of man**, the battleground, and a giver of counterfeit love, Satan is also a wiener for love, and an advocate for his brand of snake love and smoke; Satan is also prideful and arrogant, ever seeking to dethrone his **CREATOR.**

The Holy Kiss;
Jesus and Mary Magdalene

A Holy Kiss

Romans 16:16…kjv

Salute one another with an holy kiss. The churches of Christ salute you.

1 Corinthians 16:20…kjv

All the brethren greet you. Greet ye one another with an holy kiss.

11 Corinthians 13:12…kjv
Greet one another with an holy kiss.

1 Thessalonians 5:26…kjv
Greet all the brethren with an holy kiss.

*For centuries mankind's good intentions were to greet one another with a **HOLY KISS**. In many races it is common to greet one another with a heart felt kiss; even in the realms of church and governments.*

The Holy Kiss;
Jesus and Mary Magdalene

The Spirit of God only recognizes four specifics types of loves; they are Agape Love, Phileo Love, Storge Love, and Eros Love. The Spirit of God unfolds these four loves in a sequential pattern on the earth; God renders his love from heaven in the form of Agape love an then on the earth mankind unfolds the second stage of love which is Phileo. The primary love within the umbrella of the family is the Storge Love. Last, but not least, the primary love of sexual desires is explicitly reserved for a **marriage between a man and a woman**; this is Eros Love. Eros is not a random carnal love; the spirit of God rejects all lust of the flesh. Eros is a love that originates in a marriage covenant with God; especially when the virgin's hymen is broken in a spiritual and natural blood covenant for a lifetime, under grace.

God Has Four Different Kinds of Love:

1- *Agape Love is the love God has for a Man or a Woman on the earth.*
2- *Phileo Love is the love Man has for Man.*
3- *Storge Love is the Love of Sons, Daughters.*
4- *Eros Love is the love and sexual desires of Husband and Wife.*

The Holy Kiss;
Jesus and Mary Magdalene

AGAPE LOVE

Agape love is unselfish and committed love.

Agape is a love that one is willing to die for, unconditional. It has a deep respect and moral principles and for one another. It is a love even given to a complete stranger; a deep abiding love without limits.

Agape Love is not a love with conditions or merits attached to deeds; God, the father so loved us that he gave his only Son.

Matthew 22:37…kjv
Jesus said unto him, Thou shalt love the Lord thy God with all thy heart, and with all thy soul, and with all thy mind.

John 3:16…kjv
For God so loved the world, that he gave his only begotten Son, that whosoever believeth in him should not perish, but have everlasting life.

John 15:13…kjv
Greater love hath no man than this, that a man lay down his life for his friends.

The Holy Kiss;
Jesus and Mary Magdalene

PHILEO LOVE

Phileo Love is that love that draws you to be another person's friend. Phileo means brotherly love, the kind of love that Christians should have for another. It is a compound word composed of the base from "phileo" (love) and the word for "brother," adelphos. Phileo Love is the second most mentioned in the New Testament Gospels.

Reference Scripture:
Romans 12:10…kjv
Be kindly affected one to another with brotherly love; in honour preferring one another;

1st Thessalonians 4:9…kjv
But as touching brotherly love ye need not that I write unto you: for ye yourselves are taught of God to love one another.
Hebrews 13:1…kjv
Let brotherly love continue

1st Peter 1:22…kjv
Seeing ye have purified your souls in obeying the truth through the Spirit unto unfeigned love of the brethren, see that ye love on another with a pure heart fervently:

The Holy Kiss;
Jesus and Mary Magdalene

STORGE LOVE

Storge Love is a physical show of affection that results from a pure expression such as an embrace, like a hug, a kiss, or another expression of affection. Many of the ancient peoples and governments displayed this physical affection with their greetings.

Within the family circumference, Storge Love is also a love rooted within families, such as brothers and sisters, siblings, and extended family members. Storge Love is also a kind of love that a wife needs **more from her husband** than her husband needs from her.

Hence, In the spirit of God, obedience is not optional, however, it is easier to obey God and seek his kingdom first. Each of the Four Loves is directly linked to the **obedience factors** of the Father in heaven.

Romans 1:31…kjv
Without understanding, covenant breakers, without natural affection, implacable, unmerciful:

The Holy Kiss;
Jesus and Mary Magdalene

EROS LOVE

Eros Love is needed to make a marriage. Eros love fulfills the physical sexual desires of the marriage, of husband and wife. Eros love also refers to sexual passionate type love. The sexual intimacy fulfills all the emotions of love and affection of which the **Love of Eros** divinely becomes one flesh "in Christ Jesus;" unconditional love. Eros is also a love of romance. In a marriage, all four of God's Loves are essential.

Matthew 19:5,6...kjv
And said, For this cause shall a man leave father and mother, and shall cleave to his wife: and they twain shall be one Flesh? 6 Wherefore they are no more twain, but one flesh. What therefore God hath joined together, let not man put asunder.

Proverb 7:18...kjv
Come, let us take our fill of love until the morning: let us solace ourselves with loves.

To summarize, the Gnostics authors did not believe in Christ; the affection that Jesus had for Mary Magdalene was no greater than that of God's love to mankind.

Page 193
The Mystery of…Da Vinci's
Two Versions of the Madonna (s) of the Rocks

The <u>Biblical</u> Mystery…

…of Leonardo da Vinci's The Madonna (s) of the Rocks

The **Biblical** Mystery of the Madonna (s) of the Rocks

Version Number (1)
1483 – 1490 oil on wood
199 x 122 cm Paris, Musee du Louvre

Version Number (2)
ca 1490-1508 oil on wood
189.5 x 120cm London, National Gallery

Leonardo da Vinci painted two separate versions of the Madonna of the Rocks; two separate spiritual masterpieces. For centuries this mystery has been unsolved. It has been stated that the paintings are very ambiguous and why are the two versions so mismatched. Both paintings have the same depiction of the **Virgin and Christ**, *the infant child*, accompanied by **the child John the Baptist** and with an angel all grouped within a rocky cave.

The Mystery of...Da Vinci's Two Versions of the Madonna (s) of the Rocks

The paintings of the Madonna of the Rocks were of the end results of a controversial commission given to Da Vinci. This commissioned painting was from the Confraternity of the Immaculate Conception for an altar triptych, a *picture composite in three panels.*

The depictions of the panels were specified in the contract; this contract was to include and depict **God in the overhead and two side panels depicting two prophets.**. The contract also specified that the **Virgin of the Rocks** would be the centerpiece of the painting. However, these specifics were never to be, because Da Vinci deviated from the original specifications of incorporating God and the two prophets in separate paneled locations.

There again, for Da Vinci, to paint one separate prophet to the left panel and one separate prophet to the right panel at random would have been a non-sequential and unbalanced truth; instead Leonardo chose to transpose the physics of the Logos on canvas; Elohim the Thinker in the past and present tenses.

The Mystery of…Da Vinci's
Two Versions of the Madonna (s) of the Rocks

Da Vinci was a gifted genius that had the discernment of the Logos of God; God's directives of the past, the present, the future and he also understood the progressive physics of the divine mandates of the spoken word of God. Da Vinci, comprehended the divine "Order of God" and the physical manifestations of God's mandates in the progression of **_TIME_** itself.

Decoding…….

*Why are there **two versions** of this painting and why are the two versions **mismatched**?*

*The Biblical truth of Da Vinci's mysterious anomalies of the Madonna (s) of the Rocks reveals that they are…the Physics of the Logos and the Rhema of God; the encoded cosmic dynamics of **Heaven's Logos and Rhema**; the creators sequences of the Logos and the Rhema.*

The Mystery of…Da Vinci's Two Versions of the Madonna (s) of the Rocks

*Leonardo da Vinci illustrated the divine physics and the divine order of the **Logos and Rhema**; the Bookends of **Thought and Word** in visual composites; the **pre-existence and the existence** of God's ordered mandate.*

In the realm of the Third Heaven, the Physics of the Logos become the Rhema and the physics of the Rhema becomes physical manifestation on the earth; birth. The Renaissance Era understood the physics of the Bible. John 1:1,2…In the beginning was the Word, and the Word was with God, and the Word was God. 2 The same was in the beginning with God. Leonardo da Vinci knew that the physics of the logos, **thought,** *mandated the Birth of the Savior, and the supernatural physics of the* **Word,** *executed the orders of the physical. This is why Leonardo's paintings of the Madonna (s) of the Rocks are extremely enigmatic.*

The Mystery of…Da Vinci's Two Versions of the Madonna (s) of the Rocks

Leonardo used this technique of exposing the Origin of GOD'S WILL and wisdom thereof, in various spiritual paintings.

(((Logos))) & (((Rhema)))

The Logos, is the Thought, the origin thought of God, Elohim.

The Rhema, is the Word; the sent spoken word of God; hence, manifested.

The "**Thought**" of the Logos puts into existence the "**Word**" of the Rhema and the Rhema Word, mandates the birth of the physical.

The Mystery of…Da Vinci's Two Versions of the Madonna (s) of the Rocks

God's thoughts are 100%; mankind's thoughts are only 10% of the entire brain in the fallen earth. Mankind is devoid of **90% "thought."**

Isaiah 55:8,9…For my thoughts are not your thoughts, neither are your ways my ways, saith the LORD. For as the heavens are higher than the earth, so are my ways higher than your ways, and my thoughts than you thoughts.

Now, without the sequences of God's Logos and Rhema, what the Confraternity was requesting of Leonardo would have been a *Helter-Skelter composite*; hence, Da Vinci was a perfectionist to the exact true sequence of God's directives.

As his paintings reveal, Da Vinci's Biblical knowledge and wisdom was probably beyond the discerning abilities of the Confraternity of the Immaculate Conception as to Bible sequential protocol towards a **visual** Biblical layout; culminating into a condensed divine composition.

The Mystery of…Da Vinci's Two Versions of the Madonna (s) of the Rocks

Da Vinci utilized side panels in his Art as metaphors of TIME; the tangible physics of TIME. The illustration of panels for Da Vinci was a method of establishing TIME, such as a place in TIME, or the TIME of day, also as a historical moment or event in Bible history of TIME. In actuality, Leonardo da Vinci positioned the physics of TIME within his spiritual paintings.

The Madonna of the Rocks, was commissioned to be painted in separate panels as a triptych. Instead, Leonardo da Vinci brilliantly opted to paint and introduce the creation origin of **THOUGHT, the LOGOS**, and the plan for mankind's salvation. The Bible declares that all souls were with God in the beginning of TIME.

The question why Leonardo deviated from the Confraternity's origin design, we may never know, but one thing the painting tells us decisively is that Da Vinci knew the Bible and the Order of Elohim, the Logos. In John 1:14, the Logos became Rhema, flesh manifested.

John 1:14…And the Word was made flesh, and dwelt among us, (and we beheld his glory, the glory as of the only begotten of the Father,) full of grace and truth.

The Mystery of…Da Vinci's Two Versions of the Madonna (s) of the Rocks

These are the Physics of God's Mandate in the composites of the Madonna (s) of the Rocks:

The **Logos, "thought"** … first

<<< Then >>>

The **Rhema, "word"** …second

Hence, the physical manifested…….a child is born.

*Da Vinci's mystery of the two versions of the Madonna (s) of the Rocks is that they are like two **bookends**; a pair. One visual is for the **past**, The Old Testament and the other visual is for the **present**, The New Testament.*

The **Biblical** Mystery of the Madonna (s) of the Rocks,
Version Number (1)
1483 – 1490 oil on wood - 199 x 122 cm
Paris, Musee du Louvre

Decoding Data:

The first versions of the Madonna of the Rocks was painted in 1483 – 1490 oil on wood, 199 x 122 cm, Paris, Musee du Louvre. The function of this version was disputed and uncertain to this day; before this publication. This Biblical composition is the visual mandate of the Logos of heaven…….ordered for the Old Testament.

The Prelude

This version of the Madonna of the Rocks is within the **Logos of God,** *the "thought"; the mandate for the Old Testament; the mind of prophesy. Logos, is the thought, the idea, and the plan.*

The Mystery of…Da Vinci's
Two Versions of the Madonna (s) of the Rocks

Version Number (1)

The Prelude Continued…

Angels receive their commands in the realm of the Logos; angels stand in the presence of God; the presence of the Angel Uriel indicates that God is the invisible sovereign. The mystery of the Angel illustrates the presence of God in the omnipresence and omniscient powers.

The Logos of God, mandates in ***ADVANCE of the future***. God alone sees the future; God alone prototypes the future. Version No. 1 of the Madonna of the Rocks is the visual of God's "WILL", the Logos, the Thinker.

Scripture Reference:
Isaiah 55:8…for my thoughts are not your thoughts, neither are your ways my ways, saith the LORD.

This painting has been interpreted as a "legend;" stating that the infant Christ was visited in a cave or dimmed grotto by his cousin, John the Baptist, who was the same age. Through the centuries, the gestures and messages of this illustration had remained unclear and mysterious until this publication's revelation.

The Mystery of…Da Vinci's Two Versions of the Madonna (s) of the Rocks

*In this Painting, the Rocky Grotto in the cave is the realm of "**THOUGHT**", TYPES AND SHADOWS in the Third Dimension………,Heaven.*

Version Number (1): Logos; The Physics of "*thought*"

The Pre-Existence…*Elohim, The Thinker*

*In the pyramidal illustration, John the Baptist was mandated by The Lord God; the divine "ORDERS" in the realm of "**though**t," the Logos. God's directives from the "**thought**" are commanded and revealed by angels; angels DWELL in the presence of the God Head. This <u>Version No.1</u>, is the visual of the "**thought**" within the sovereign source and origin command of the Spirit of God… John the Baptist was mandated for the future and angels **executes forth** God's ORDERS; John the Baptist in the painting is the forerunner before the BLOOD.*

The Mystery of…Da Vinci's Two Versions of the Madonna (s) of the Rocks

*For over 500 years, the greatest unknown mystery of Da Vinci in <u>Version No. 1</u> of the Madonna of the Rocks is the enigmatic **<u>authoritative hand gestures</u>** of the Christ Child, the Angel, and the Madonna; all are grouped to the right of the composition. The mystery reveals **<u>The Word within the Logos</u>**, rendering blessings and commanding salvation for the earth. The Virgin's hand gesture, while embracing John the Baptist, receives the Mind of Christ.*

<u>Logos Scripture Reference:</u>
Jeremiah 1:5…Before I formed thee in the belly I knew thee; and before thou camest forth out of the womb I sanctified thee, and I ordained thee a prophet unto the nations.

Jeremiah 29:11…kjv
For I know the thoughts that think toward you, saith the LORD, thoughts of peace, and not of evil, to give you an expected end.

The Mystery of…Da Vinci's Two Versions of the Madonna (s) of the Rocks

Decoding…in the realm of "__thought__," Da Vinci's Biblical Logos on Canvas

(1) <u>In Version No. 1</u>, of the Madonna of the Rocks, the Christ Child is authorizing and blessing John the Baptist; forerunner of Salvation. The rocky grotto, is indicative of the secret place of God; Logos; *Psalm 18:11…He made darkness his secret place; his pavilion round about him were dark waters and thick clouds of the skies.*

(2) In the grotto, the Angel is positioned in the presence of God; the Angel is advertent, receiving and enforcing God's directive, ORDERS. The angel's authoritative hand-pointing gesture, activates the culmination and manifestation of the Rhema; the chosen vessel that of John the Baptist.

(3) In this grotto, the Madonna, who is pre-destined, is embracing John the Baptist; their embrace to the left of the painting, is the pre-manifestation for the earth, which **captures** the authority of the Angel's <u>ORDERS</u> and the **Word of the Christ**, these are the dualistic directives from the right of the painting.

The Mystery of…Da Vinci's Two Versions of the Madonna (s) of the Rocks

Decoding…in the realm of "***thought***", Da Vinci's Biblical Logos on Canvas

For centuries the mystery of the Virgin raising one hand above the Angel's pointed-directives has remained unsolved until this publication; **the Virgin is given this authority because mankind shares the Mind of Christ, not angels**. In this painting, the Angel comes from the Logos, "***thought,***" and the Christ Child is the Word of God, hence, The Lord God. The Word of the Christ is a **_Sent Word,_** which blesses the Virgin and John the Baptist who are pre-destined to the earth. The Virgin and John the Baptist, **together**, hold the ultimate and everlasting authority over the angels of heaven because angels do not have the **_MIND of CHRIST_**; only mankind has the mind of Christ; only mankind was given the gift of "***thought and reason***" from the origin source, Elohim. Da Vinci undisputedly knew the Logos and the Rhema of God.

Mankind: The Heirs of Salvation, not Angels

Hebrew 1:13,14…But to which of the angels said he at any time, Sit on my right hand, until I make thine enemies thy footstool? 14 Are they not all ministering spirits, sent forth to mister for them who shall be heirs of salvation?

The Mystery of…Da Vinci's Two Versions of the Madonna (s) of the Rocks

ANGELS STAND IN THE PRESENCE OF GOD:

In the New Testament, the Angel Gabriel was ordered by God to speak to Zacharias, a Levitical Priest, that his wife Elisabeth will bear a son, and his name will be John.

Reference Scriptures

Luke 1:5,6,7…There was in the days of Herod, the king of Judaea, a certain priest named Zacharias, of the course of Abia: and his wife was of the daughters of Aaron, and her name was Elisabeth. 6 And they were both righteous before God, walking in all the commandments and ordinances of the Lord blameless. 7 And they had no child, because that Elisabeth was barren, and they both were now well stricken in years.

Luke 1:11,13…And there appeared unto him an angel of the Lord standing on the right side of theater of incense. 13 But the angel said unto him, Fear not, Zacharias: for they prayer is heard; and they wife Elisabeth shall bear thee a son, and thou shalt call his name John.

Luke 1:19…And the angel answering said unto him, I am Gabriel, that stand in the presence of God; and am sent to speak unto thee, and to show thee these glad tidings.

The Mystery of...Da Vinci's Two Versions of the Madonna (s) of the Rocks

*Decoding...in the realm of "**thought**", Da Vinci's Biblical Logos on Canvas*

(4) Angels only serve the directives from the MIND OF THE LOGOS, "**thought**."

Wisdom………On the earth, rockets and bombs cannot blow up an Angel, of course, but angels escort war weapons towards the permissive "WILL OF GOD." Angels do not have the Mind of Christ; only mankind has the Mind of Christ from the origin of the Logos. Angels cannot be seated at the right hand of the father. Angels do not know God's inner thoughts until they receive their Orders from the Logos. Angels are our servants, Angels are also curious of "**thought**."

*Angels Desire: 1st Peter 1:12…Unto whom it was revealed, that not unto themselves, but unto us they did minister the things, which are now reported unto you by them that have preached the gospel unto you with the Holy Ghost sent down from heaven; which things the angels desire to **look into**.*

(5) In the Rocky Grotto, also the Christ Child is unclothed with Elohim; the Christ is authorizing John the Baptist, while he sits on the metaphor of solid rock; thence, the Blood to come*; Psalm 28:1…Unto thee will I cry, O LORD my rock.*

The Mystery of…Da Vinci's Two Versions of the Madonna (s) of the Rocks

*Decoding…in the realm of "**thought**", Da Vinci's Biblical Logos on Canvas*

Continuing…(5)

Also, in this Version No.1, the Christ Child is sitting under the Angel's command, because scripture declares that Christ was made lower than the Angels.

Psalm 8:5…For thou has made him a little lower than the angels, and hast crowned him with glory and honour.

(6)   Also, the Christ Child in <u>Version No. 1</u> is physically portrayed more linear and slender in body weight in this first grotto composition, because the perspective image of the Christ Child still dwells within the Logos, "***thought***," and he has not yet been manifested in the physics of the earth's flesh; the Rhema. However, **In Version No. 2**, of the Madonna of the Rocks, Da Vinci, then… renders the second perspective of the flesh manifested on the earth with a more plump and stoutly Christ Child.

The Mystery of…Da Vinci's Two Versions of the Madonna (s) of the Rocks

*Decoding…in the realm of "**thought**", Da Vinci's Biblical Logos on Canvas*

Continuing…(6)

Leonardo da Vinci frequently used this mysterious body weight technique in his various motifs to illustrate the **contrast of the Spirit and the Flesh**; two separate realms. These motifs of stoutly and/or slender body images of Da Vinci's infant composites, reveal a unique code that signifies the two interpretations of **The Spirit Realm verses the Earthly Realm**; two distinctive domains of spiritual powers.

Decoding………

The Madonna of the Rocks, Version No. 1, introduces the **chosen vessels** for the salvation plan for the earth. The Virgin and John the Baptist are the two **earthly figures chosen** to fulfill heaven's plan; this is why the Madonna is embracing John the Baptist because she is the Salvation's vessel chosen to bring forth the savior and John is the forerunner of Salvation's mandate. In this Version No. 1, the Angel is in the presence of God receiving and directing the mandate from the Logos.

The Mystery of…Da Vinci's Two Versions of the Madonna (s) of the Rocks

*Decoding…in the realm of "**thought**", Da Vinci's Biblical Logos on Canvas*

To reiterate, to the **Right** of the painting, the Virgin is the vessel of the Christ Child and she is giving the **authoritative hand gesture** above the angel's directives because angels **do not and cannot** possess the mind of Christ. Da Vinci, used the language of the hands to illustrate the executed Commands and Orders of God. The Right of this painting transcends the triple dimensions of spiritual rank and file and authorities within the "***thought***" of the Logos.

It must be noted that after Adam and Eve sinned, angels **took authority**; hence, in Genesis an angel with the flaming sword took control and authority of the Tree of the Knowledge of Good and Evil.

SUMMARY:

*The Madonna of the Rocks, <u>Versions No. 1</u>…The Redemptive Plan in the "**thought**" of the Logos*

*In the painting, **The Angel and The Lord** are within the presence of God in the Logos dominance of Elohim, the visual "**thought**" of heaven's mandate for mankind's Salvation.*

The Mystery of…Da Vinci's
Two Versions of the Madonna (s) of the Rocks

SUMMARY CONTINUED:
*The Madonna of the Rocks, Versions No. 1…The Redemptive Plan in the "**thought**" of the Logos*

To the Left…of the painting, Da Vinci also illustrates <u>The Virgin and The Baptist</u> who are pre-destined by the Godhead into the future. . The Virgin and the Baptist were ordered for the EARTH within the dimensions of the Logos. The Virgin and the Baptist are the two pre-destined earthbound authorities spiritually commanded from heaven's realm. In the beginning was the Word within the Logos; "**thought.**"

John 1:1… In the beginning was the Word, and the word was with God, and the Word was God. . 2 The same was in the beginning with God.

On the earth, governments inherit all the divine logistics of God as it pertains to mandates, commands, and/or execution thereof. **But** in heaven, the angels enforce all three directives; God is omnipresent and the angels are the warriors, guardians, and messengers. The Divine Command Headquarters of Heaven, encircles the pre-destined spiritual prototypes…, types and shadows, also the "**thought**" and directives, hence, the Logos.

The Mystery of…Da Vinci's Two Versions of the Madonna (s) of the Rocks

*Decoding…in the realm of "**thought**", Da Vinci's Biblical Logos on Canvas*

Leonardo da Vinci's genius, spanned beyond the reach of Albert Einstein, Galileo, and Newton, because he possessed the intellect and wisdom of **GOD WITH SCIENCE,** ever present; Da Vinci had knowledge and wisdom of God and the Mind; the conscience thereof. BUT, Einstein, Galileo, Newton, and even Charles Darwin's vital missing links, isolated themselves within the **stationary pendulum** of the directives of God; the directives of the universe which are the sciences thereof.

Leonardo da Vinci, knew and understood that God was the creator, the "mover" and "shaker" of everything; everything. Da Vinci comprehended and visualized the intelligent designer, the thinker and his hosts of angels, and provider of salvation; eternal life.

Through the power of the Holy Spirit, the righteous receive wisdom from God; but the unrighteous, and the unsaved, and the chastised, receive the intellects of the world, <u>coupled</u> with uncertainties, doubt, denials, stagnation, fears, vengeance, religions, and denominational legalism, all from the daily Spiritual War; within the fallen earth.

Page 215
The Mystery of…Da Vinci's Two Versions of the Madonna (s) of the Rocks

Decoding…in the realm of "__thought__", Da Vinci's Biblical Logos on Canvas

Da Vinci knew that without the wisdom of God, "**intellect and reason**" just meanders below the clouds, rebounding throughout the four cardinal directions, repeating the blunders of history.

*For centuries, mankind's "intellect" has analyzed and searched for "Cause and Effect," but the universe of God is, "__**Thought, Cause, and Effect**__;" the Logos, Elohim. The Logos of the Big Bang.*

?……Who is man that he thinketh that "**thought**" was his own?

?……Who is man that only thinketh with "**ten percent**" of heaven's electromagnetic-spark; God's celestial realm?

Thence, Luke 10:18…And he said unto them, I beheld Satan as lightning fall from heaven.

The Mystery of…Da Vinci's
Two Versions of the Madonna (s) of the Rocks

Discernment of "**thought:**"

God is the "thought" and creator of the universe, cosmos. Psalm 19:1…the heavens declare the glory of God; and the firmament showeth his handiwork.

God is the origin of "**thought**." Mankind extracts "**thought**" from the Logos. Nothing, nothing,…just happens without the knowledge and "**will**" of God.
Why is God omnipotent and omniscient??? Because God's "thoughts" are always ahead of mankind's **miniscule** (10%) equation of "thought." God's Spirit, all knowing and omnipresent, has always existed; the origin of "thought" is ingrained in logistical SPIRITUAL ORDER.

The complex irony of human "**thought**" is that mankind's miniscule equation is always, always…, spiritually programmed **behind the advanced** "**thoughts**" of God; Human "**thought**" perpetually resides within the omnipotent and omnipresent powers of God. God's infinite "thoughts" are propelled in advance of the mind of man; In other words, God knows humanity's "**thoughts**" in advance and prior to our future.

Two Versions of the Madonna (s) of the Rocks
…Da Vinci Studied the Logos

Continued…

Discernment of "**thought:**"

Heaven's divine dominance of **forward "thought"** renders the pivotal physics of the omnipresent and omniscient factors which allows the Spirit of God to foresee the infinite future of mankind and the entire cosmos. God's camera develops in the darkness.

Another universal reason why the Lord God is the almighty King of Kings and Lord of Lords, is because the entity of EVIL, *Satan*, does not possess the physics of "**thought.**" The powers of Satan are **only** conjoined to the mind of man; the mind of "choice." Satan cannot extract "**thought and reason**" from the Animal Kingdom; the animals belong to a separate inherent kingdom of the instinctual properties in the physic of the WILD. The Animal Kingdom does not have dominion over the earth; mankind and his dominion is the only lucrative spiritual value of Satan's deceptions; in other words, Satan cannot deceive a beast of the field. In the Book of Daniel 4:31, the "**Logos**" of heaven plunged the arrogant king Nebuchadnezzar into the realm of the beasts, (animal kingdom) for exalting his "**diminutive physics of "thought"** over the "**THOUGHT" circuitry of heaven's Logos**; the sovereign God.

Two Versions of the Madonna (s) of the Rocks
…Da Vinci Studied the Logos

Continued…

Discernment of "<u>thought:</u>"

God, the most High Elohim, sequestered King Nebuchadnezzar's "**thoughts**" within the delirium of the physics of the "WILD" for seven years and nocturnal existence thereof, *Daniel 4:33*. "The physics of ***"THOUGHT"* IS NOT NOCTURNAL."**

Scripture Reference:

Daniel 4:30,31,32,33…The king spake, and said, Is not this great Babylon, that I have built for the house of the kingdom by the might of my power, and for the honour of my majesty? While the word was in the king's mouth, there fell a voice from heaven, saying, O king Nebuchadnezzar, to thee it is spoken; The kingdom is departed from thee. And they shall drive thee from men, and thy dwelling shall be with the beasts of the field: they shall make thee to eat grass as oxen, and seven times shall pass over thee, until thou know that the most High ruleth in the kingdom of men, and giveth it to whomsoever he will. The same hour was the thing fulfilled upon Nebuchadnezzar: and he was driven from men, and did eat grass as oxen, and his body was wet with the dew of heaven, till his hairs were grown like eagles' feathers, and his nails like birds' claws.

Two Versions of the Madonna (s) of the Rocks
…Da Vinci Studied the Logos

Continued…

Discernment of "**thought**:"

Satan's powers of choice and dominion were stripped in the catastrophic and cataclysmic overthrow, eviction, from the domain of the 3rd heaven. Satan's capacity is limited by way of deception of mankind's processes of "thought and reason," which Biblically is the Spiritual Battle for the Mind; post Adam and Eve.

From the foundations of the heavens, "**thought**" is the inherent engine of the properties of God, of which man has been given a 10% inheritence. Throughout the entire universe, only God and man share "**thought**," angels and demons do not have the power of "**thought**" and choice…; free-will.

Only God, the Logos, and mankind share the physics of "**thought**." **The Provision of Christ,** filters out the deceptions of evil which contaminates righteousness. The origin of **"thought"** is an intelligent "ORDER" of logic, reason, perfection, and righteousness; Elohim. The universe only has one truth. The provision of Christ, is the only truth and power which renders wisdom to the mind of man.

Two Versions of the Madonna (s) of the Rocks
…Da Vinci Studied the Logos

Continued…

Discernment of "**thought**:

"Thought," existed before Space and Time…Elohim
"Thought," existed before Energy and Matter…Logos
"Thought," existed before Iniquity,……Lucifer=1/3 hosts
"Thought," existed before Sin,……Adam and Eve.
        Satan attacks the framework of "thought."

Discernment of "**thought**;" without Satan's Entity:

Satan bids for "mankind's "**thoughts**" against the righteous structure of world governments, thrones, doctrines of religions, and against the truth of Christ. Satan does not possess the properties of "**thought**", he utilizes mankind's framework of "thought and reason" against God; also, Satan cannot read your **"thoughts" unless a person is possessed with demons**, as in Mary Magdalene.

Two Versions of the Madonna (s) of the Rocks
...Da Vinci Studied the Logos

Continued...

Discernment of "**thought;**" without Satan's Entity:

However, Satan does hear the authority and the power of the tongue; death and life are in the power of the tongue. God is the only sovereign power that knows man's "**thoughts**," but Satan **cannot** read "**thought**" UNLESS, the person is possessed with Satan and/or his demons. Once, a person's mind, body, and soul is demonically possessed, their concepts of "thinking" and desires of "**thought**" are invaded and become known by a three-way channel; *God, the possessed, and Satan*. This is why the spiritual process of exorcisms is lacking in knowledge to the world. "*Thought*" is a spiritual by-product of the Logos; thinker.

The deceiver challenges "**mankind's thoughts**," against the origin of the "**thinker**," the Logos. Even during the Flood of Noah when eight righteous people entered the Ark and the waters prevailed and covered the mountains; subsequently, the spirit of **EVIL** although dormant, still had authority within the physics of "**thought and reason of the mind,**" within the fallen earth. Hence, Canaan...... Genesis 9:25; Satan is the deceiver of the mind, he is the historical mythical dragon of the eons.

Two Versions of the Madonna (s) of the Rocks
…Da Vinci Studied the Logos

Continued…

Discernment of "**thought**;" without Satan's Entity:

*The CONSCIENCE…The awareness of right and wrong in the "**thought processes**" within the brain.*

The divine component of the "thought" is called the conscience, because we are of God, we are but a smatter of the origin of "thought;" Elohim. The etymology of the word "*conscience*" means that mankind's "**thought and reason**" are with creation science, Logos and Creator.

In the Garden of Eden:

BEFORE SIN……it was God "the thinker" and Adam, the "thought."

In the beginning "the thinker" who is the Godhead known as the Elohim, said "Let us make man." This man was called Adam the "**thought**" of God; who was also given the attribute and inherent physics of God the Logos.

BEFORE SIN……. Adam's "**thoughts**" knew "NO EVIL."

BEFORE SIN……Adam's "**thought and reason**" named every living creature; his dominion thereof, Genesis 2:19.

Two Versions of the Madonna (s) of the Rocks
…Da Vinci Studied the Logos

Continued…

Discernment of "**thought;**" without Satan's Entity:

<u>In the Garden of Eden,</u> Satan came in as a beast of the field; Satan was cleaver, he knew that God gave man dominion over the earth and the beasts of the field. Satan, a.k.a., Lucifer treasured the gift of free-will; Satan knew of the universal awesome powers of "**CHOICE**," *free-will,* which was given to the inheritance of Adam and Eve. Eons before, Satan relished the powers of dominion over the earth, which God had given him before his cosmic and cataclysmic **EVICTION**, for arrogance and pride; hence, God cut him down into a dormant demise.

AFTER SIN……the domain of the conscience suffered the foreign dominance and deceptions with Evil's progressive authority; Adam and Eve's disobedience against God.

AFTER SIN……Adam's "**thoughts**" revealed to him that he was afraid and naked, Genesis 3:10.

AFTER SIN……. the spirit of EVIL, Satan, gained coalesced existence with "**thought**," through the free-will agents of Adam and Eve.

Two Versions of the Madonna (s) of the Rocks
…Da Vinci Studied the Logos

Leonardo da Vinci, understood the creation science of God's advanced and FIXED-AXIS of "**thought**," the Logos; God's advanced "**thought**" over man, allows him to measure and search the heart; the reins of the flesh……..

*Jeremiah 17:9,10…The heart is deceitful above all things, and desperately wicked: who can know it? I The LORD search the heart, **I try the reins**, even to give every man according to his ways, and according to the fruit of his doings.*

God allows "EVIL" to infiltrate the physics of the established nature of "thought and reason." However, "evil" can freely be rebuked if one seeks the Kingdom of God and the Mind of Christ. "Evil," can be rebuked because it is not a component of the origin **hard-drive or database of "thought."** Before the existence of EVIL, "**thought**" was. Our **Brain Waves** are of the creation physics of the Logos not genetics or D.N.A. of the **flesh**; the electro-sparks of the mind are of the Creator, Elohim.

In the Garden of Eden, it was God and Adam, they were the two communicative "**thinkers**" of the earth. God, the thinker, and Adam was God's "*__thought__*;" the origin of…*Genesis 1:26… And God said, Let us make man in our image after our likeness:*

Two Versions of the Madonna (s) of the Rocks
…Da Vinci Studied the Logos

The "**Thought Physics**" of the Godhead in the Earth's Geniuses…and the Savant Genius Factors:

All the sciences get their **commands** and directives from God. Spiritually and scientifically the sovereign components and properties of the Divine Godhead of heaven are as follows:

The essence of **GENIUS** derives from the Spiritual Physics of the Logos…the intelligent source of divine "***thought***." There are three separate isolated spiritual physics of GENIUS FACTORS in the earth.

(1) **A Nature Genius**…Born and gifted with an astounding depth of intelligence and reasoning; a near perfect advanced balance of the entire brain and mind; some Nature Geniuses acquire or adapt a healthy introvert behavior; they are profound "*thinkers.*"

(2) **Visual Genius**…Born, but later mentally traumatized and blessed with a **Genius Facet** of the visuals and sciences thereof. In such traumas, the brain and the memory reverts and transcends forth…to extract the origin intelligence within the Logos; thus inheriting depth of dimensions and divine perspective.

Two Versions of the Madonna (s) of the Rocks
…Da Vinci Studied the Logos

The "**Thought Physics**" of the Godhead in the Earth's Geniuses…and the Savant Genius Factors:

(3) **Born a Savant**… and blessed with the divine gifts from the Logos; they inherit segmented **Genius Facets** of mathematics, memory, and equations,… but without the perfection of **speech**. A Savant is gifted with segments of God's extended perfection from the 99.999999999% database of heaven's supernatural intelligence…., But however, not in language, physical skills, and speech. A Savant also masters ownership of the **Physics of Music**, because the Gift of Music was given to mankind **after** the Archangel Lucifer, Angel of Music, was cut to the ground, the earth. Lucifer was the complete dominant factor of the science of **MUSIC** before he was evicted from the THIRD HEAVEN.

The Logos…The properties of the Logos are as follows:

The Logos is the spiritual component of the origin of the "*electro-spark of thought*," the Logos, is the visual perspective and cosmic geometric within the radius…, types and shadows thereof, and the database of **"*memory*"** and **"*thought*"** dominance, hence, the conscience; the Father God.

Two Versions of the Madonna (s) of the Rocks
…Da Vinci Studied the Logos

The "**Thought Physics**" of the Godhead in the Earth's Geniuses…and the Savants Genius Factors:

The Rhema…The properties of the Rhema are as follows:

The Rhema of the Godhead is the spiritual component of Language, The Word within the Lord, the Flesh, Voice… manifested sent word, and Physics of Speech; also the substance and dominance of all creation, substance of the natural, light, and nocturnal defenses.

There are three spiritual components of the **Godhead**…they are: The Logos with the Host of Angels,….The Rhema,… and The Righteous Conscience within mankind. Satan, the author of evil, terror, hatred, and confusion resides outside of the Godhead.

"The best laid plans of mice and men often go astray"

……Hence, because the earth dwells in **Spiritual War** with the agents of free-will; the mind of man. Mankind borrows "**thought**" from the origin of the Divine Logos.

Two Versions of the Madonna (s) of the Rocks
…Da Vinci Studied the Logos

The Godhead of the Logos verses
The Scientific Theory of "__Thought__"

How does the "__LOGOS__" of God equate with the scientific theory of Time Travel?

>>>>>>>>>>>>>>>>>>
<<<<<<<<<<<<<<<<<<

The Grandfather Paradox of Science…
The Grandfather Paradox of the "__Thought__"

The grandfather paradox is a scientific paradox of **Time Travel**. One of the most powerful theories introduced to the physics of "Time Travel," reveals that it could be possible to travel into the past, *(if you were so inclined)* and kill your grandfather when he was a very young child, which would render your own birth impossible.

Biblically and scientifically a person cannot travel back into "TIME" and kill his biological grandfather because the celestial powers of "__thought__," within God the Logos, can never be reversed against the appointed pre-destined "TIME" of one family's generations. Infinite **"__thought__"** is set-forth in 'TIME' and in advance of finite **"__thought__."**

Two Versions of the Madonna (s) of the Rocks
...Da Vinci Studied the Logos

Continued...

The Grandfather Paradox of Science...
The Grandfather Paradox of "<u>Thought</u>:"

Finite, "**thought and reason**" is a mere "**ten percent**" of the Logos, which is the mind of God. The paradox of **Time Travel** cannot recalibrate a pre-destined birth by the sovereignty of the cosmos. However, if a man's desires of the heart equate towards a yearning fixation for **Time Travel**, and the experiences thereof; God's permissive "WILL," will allow the influences of exploration. Since man is a free-agent, God will allow the prospects of **Time Travel** to suffereth the mind into delusions and/or illusions of numeric dimensions with *Time and Memory*, given way to limbo dimensions and "thought gymnastics" within the neurons of the brain.

The Grandfather Paradox, **<u>if it were possible</u>**, would also stand to reverse the DEEDS OF MAN within the generation of the hypothetical **Time Travel**, which is spiritually impossible because the accountability and demerits of sin... and merits and blessings of eternal life cannot be redirected into oblivion.

Two Versions of the Madonna (s) of the Rocks
...Da Vinci Studied the Logos

Continued...

The Grandfather Paradox of Science...
The Grandfather Paradox of "**Thought**:"

The structure of "**thought**" is the nucleus of the Logos, and the *memory* of the universe. Satan cannot manipulate memory. Also the types and shadows of "**Thought**," has always existed.

The infinite powers of the Logos, "**thought**," abides and resides in the Third Heaven (3rd), the celestial realm of space and time of the universe. All wisdom and supreme intelligence are exerted and conveyed through the cosmic directives of God.

In the Theory of Evolution, Charles Darwin's Natural Selection has **three pivotal missing links**. One of those major missing links is the universe's dominant **Physics of "Thought**." "**Thought**" origin equates @ 99.999999999 to the progressiveness of the Eons of "Time." The tempo of "Time" is limited; "Time" itself is paralleled with the physics of "**Thought**" and its mathematical sovereignty. Even the genius Leonardo da Vinci perfectly understood the archetypal and sequential origins of "**THOUGHT**" *with* "Time."

Page 231
Two Versions of the Madonna (s) of the Rocks
…Da Vinci Studied the Logos

*How does the "<u>LOGOS</u>" of God equate with the scientific theory of <u>**The Twin Paradox**</u>?*

The "Twin Paradox" in the Celestial:

"**<u>Thought:</u>**" The same Sovereign Rule of God directly equates to the "Twin Paradox in Time." If one twin is sent into space on a rocket and the another twin stays on the earth; the twin in space stays younger than the twin brother on the earth after the journey.

The twin in the spaceship entering the celestial realm, in essence, resists *<u>"time" against "thought,"</u>* while entering the third dimension of heaven, the Godhead.

In the journey, the past tense of "**thought**," (*finite man*), encroaches the celestial present tenses of the origin of "<u>**THOUGHT**</u>," (*infinite creator*).

This celestial and dimensional journey infiltrates and overlaps the **<u>Finite Physics of "thought;" 10%,</u>** with the **<u>Infinite Physics of Logos "Thought" within Infinity</u>**; hence the past tense and the present tense of "**thought**," <u>hesitates</u> that person's physics of "TIME," the progressiveness thereof, rendering the voyager **<u>YOUNGER IN "TIME."</u>**

Two Versions of the Madonna (s) of the Rocks
…Da Vinci Studied the Logos

Reference Scriptures:
Thinker, Thought, and Thinketh

Psalm 40:17 But I am poor and needy; yet the Lord thinketh upon me: thou art my help and my deliverer; make no tarring, O my God.

Proverb 23:7…For as he thinketh in his heart, so is he: Eat and drink, saith he to thee; but his heart is not with thee.

Galatians 6: 3…For if a man think himself to be something, when he is nothing, he deceiveth himself.

Jeremiah 29:11 For I know the thoughts that I think toward you, saith the LORD, thoughts of peace, and not of evil, to give you an expected end.

Matthew 9:4…And Jesus knowing their thoughts said, Wherefore think ye evil in your heart?

1st Corinthians 8:2.. And if any man think that he knoweth any thing, he knoweth nothing yet as he ought to know.

The Mystery of…Da Vinci's
Two Versions of the Madonna (s) of the Rocks

Continuing…

DECODING…The Madonna of the Rocks, <u>Version No. 1</u>, Biblically

DECODING…The Madonna of the Rocks, <u>Version No. 2</u>, Biblically

<u>THE SET OF TWO</u>:
<u>Version No. 1</u> is the companion of <u>Version No. 2</u>; they are a Pair of spiritual bookends. One is the **"thought"** of Heaven, Elohim, and the other is the sent word of the **"<u>physical manifestation</u>"** for the Earth.

The Mystery of…Da Vinci's
Two Versions of the Madonna (s) of the Rocks

The <u>Biblical</u> Mystery of the Madonna (s) of the Rocks, Version Number (2)

ca 1490-1508 oil on wood   -   189.5 x 120cm
London, National Gallery

<u>Decoding Data</u>:

The second version of the Madonna of the Rocks was painted in 1490 - 1508 oil on wood, 189.5 x 120cm, London, National Gallery. It has been stated that <u>Version No. 2</u> of this painting is also still a <u>riddle</u> to this present day and that it is very mysterious to understand. As I have stated, this Biblical composition is the visual **<u>Rhema of the WORD</u>** for the New Testament. This is Da Vinci's interpretation of the manifested plan on the earth; divinity thereof. Biblically, the WORD is the Rhema which is a specific sent word; a right-now word; spoken word, which angels carry out.

Unlike Version No. 1 of the Madonna of the Rocks, which Da Vinci portrayed in the "**<u>thought</u>**," secret places of Elohim; **<u>Version No. 2</u>** illustrates the substance and physical manifestation of Version No. 1 directives; ***Christ is Come in <u>the FLESH</u>***.

The Mystery of…Da Vinci's two versions of the Madonna (s) of the Rocks

In this Painting, the Grotto depicts the manifested **_life, light, and grace_** in the dimensional realm of the "**Rhema**," the sent word which was conceived in the PHYSICAL for the Earth; the earth is the first (1st) Heaven. God has rendered the earth the provision for eternal life.

Version Number (2): Rhema, the Manifested Physics

The Physical Existence…The Sent Word

*The "Sent Word" is the fulfillment and manifested "**thought**" from heaven unto the earth.*

This version of the Madonna of the Rocks is within the "**Rhema" of the Lord**, the word; the sword, and the executed orders for the New Testament; the "**thought**," physics of the Logos. To reiterate, Version Number 1, was ordered and placed into prophesy and, hence, existence. Angels always stand in the **three-fold presence of God**.

The Mystery of…Da Vinci's
Two Versions of the Madonna (s) of the Rocks

Version Number (2): Rhema, the Manifested Physics

The Physical Existence…The Sent Word

*In this <u>Version No. 2</u> of the Madonna of the Rocks, it reveals the spectrum of the "**<u>Rhema</u>**;" light and life for Salvation; light and color are emphasized.*

This second painting of Leonardo da Vinci is the physical realm, manifested on the earth; it is life and light embodied in the flesh. Before this publication, most of Da Vinci's spiritual compositions were mysterious and lacked world interpretation, because the core of Da Vinci's Biblical works involved the intricate dimensional powers of God, Elohim; the powers of creation science within the Logos and Rhema.

The Mystery of…Da Vinci's
Two Versions of the Madonna (s) of the Rocks

Decoding…in the realm of the "physical manifestation;" Da Vinci's Rhema on Canvas

(1) In this Version No. 2 of the Madonna of the Rocks, Da Vinci and his workshop painted the companion composite to the Logos. The "**Logos**" catapults the "**Rhema**" into being, existence; the physics of the physical.

This second painting reveals the earthly manifestation of the "**Rhema**" and the ***Spiritual Continuum*** of the "**Logos**," mandate on the earth.

The two paintings, **together**, illustrate the zenith of the working structural nucleus of the spiritual commands within the Spirit of God. It is the quantum, *measurable whole*, of the God Head and his directives for salvation. The Renaissance Master Artists, undoubtedly knew the Biblical nucleus of the command structure of the Spirit of the Trinity; Godhead.

The Mystery of…Da Vinci's Two Versions of the Madonna (s) of the Rocks

Decoding…in the realm of the "<u>physical manifestation</u>;" Da Vinci's Rhema on Canvas

(2)　In this <u>Version No. 2</u> of the Madonna of the Rocks, the peaceful and tranquil Angel has already fulfilled the command of the "**Logos**" into the "**Rhema**". The earlier pointed-gesture of God's directives with the Angel, have already come to fruition on the earth; which was the Angel's executed ORDERS within the Host of Hosts; the Logos. Furthermore, the Angel's continued presence represents the invisible **omnipresence** of the Spirit of God. The landscape of the <u>Version No. 2</u>, reveal the images and spectrum of light and life, emphasized within the earth's properties; creations thereof.

<u>THE INFANT CHRIST…, "IS COME IN THE FLESH"</u>

(3)　In this second version, John the Baptist and the Virgin are again **blessed** on the earth, the "Rhema," by the threefold divine powers of the omnipresence of God and Hosts, the Christ Child, and the Holy Spirit; the beautiful halos, in this painting, also illustrates the manifested blessing of heaven's chosen vessels upon the earth with the Holy Spirit. The depictions of Halos render divine authority on the earth.

The Mystery of…Da Vinci's Two Versions of the Madonna (s) of the Rocks

Decoding…in the realm of the "<u>physical manifestation;</u>" Da Vinci's Rhema on Canvas

4   In the fullness of time; Christ is come in the FLESH; Salvation cometh to the earth; John the Baptist was much more than a prophet; he was the forerunner for heaven's mandate of eternal life and the Lord's cousin.   In this painting the Baptist, is manifested by the "**<u>Rhema</u>**" with the authorities of **<u>Heaven's Staff</u>**, the **<u>Holy Spirit</u>** in him, and the wisdom of the **<u>Mind of Christ.</u>**

In this <u>Version NO. 2</u>…The Christ is the **Word of God** and the Angel is with the invisible **God the Logos**, these are the two spiritual components that constitute **"The Lord God."** The Rhema of the Christ Child enforces the twofold mandate of the Godhead; it is a simultaneous spiritual structure of command. The Virgin's hand gesture circularly affirms heaven's blessing and the Mind of Christ.

In the procedural maneuvers of world governments, the military is activated with commands and Orders, all which are executed within separate branches of authorities.

The Mystery of…Da Vinci's Two Versions of the Madonna (s) of the Rocks

Decoding…in the realm of the "<u>physical manifestation;</u>" Da Vinci's Rhema on Canvas

These "**commands**" and "**orders**" are then expedited within an allotment of time and space; but the supreme powers of the Sovereign God of the universe simultaneously commands the Logos… to the Rhema… **prior and in advance** of man's "**10% "thought physics.**" Once, God's "Will" leaves the database of the "**Logos thoughts**," all the realms of the celestial Godhead expedite HEAVEN'S ORDERS.

God has two "WILLS," the <u>PERFECT WILL</u> of God and the <u>PERMISSIVE WILL</u> of God, which inherently encompass the "**thought physics**" of the Logos.

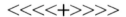

*The spectrum of color and light that Da Vinci and his workshop gave the **RHEMA** of the Madonna of the Rocks, <u>Version No. 2</u>, illustrates the divine sovereign authority and mandate of Heaven on the Earth.*

The Mystery of…Da Vinci's
Two Versions of the Madonna (s) of the Rocks

Decoding…in the realm of the "physical manifestation;" Da Vinci's Rhema on Canvas

(5)   THE CLOCKWISE ENIGMA:

Spiritually both composites have a clockwise theory; the hypothesis of the Earth's Clock. Both paintings depict the same anatomical positions and the same numeric direction as the hands of a clock. The paintings have the analogical positions of a numerical course, as the movement of the hands of a clock; clockwise.

Within the Circumference of the Virgin, the Baptist, the Angel and the Christ, the numerics are as follows:

1-   *The Virgin is positioned at 12:00 O' Clock and at 6:00 O'Clock.*

2-   *The Christ Child who is conjoined to the Host of the Angels, the Godhead, is positioned at 3:00 O'Clock.*

3-   *The Baptist, John, is positioned at 9:00 O'Clock.*

Here again, Leonardo da Vinci encoded the presence of "TIME," and existence thereof.

The Mystery of…Da Vinci's
Two Versions of the Madonna (s) of the Rocks

Version Number (2)

*<u>Version No.</u> 2 of the Madonna of the Rocks establishes the "**<u>Rhema</u>**," it is the <u>fates of completion</u> from the origin of the "WILL" of God; the divine WILL within the origin of the Logos, which is beyond human control, the **<u>SENT WORD</u>** known as the "**<u>Rhema</u>**."*

<u>Some scriptures in reference:</u>

<u>Reference: A Specific Word</u>
Acts 10:36…The word which God sent unto the children of Israel, preaching peace by Jesus Christ: (he is Lord of all:)

<u>Reference: The Word</u>
John 1:1…In the beginning was the Word, and the Word was with God, and the Word was God. 2 The same was in the beginning with God.

The Mystery of…Da Vinci's Two Versions of the Madonna (s) of the Rocks

Some scriptures in reference:

Reference: The Spoken Word

Ephesians 6:17…And take the helmet of Salvation, and the sword of the Spirit which is the word of God.

Reference: The Sent Word

Isaiah 55:11…So shall my word be that goeth forth out of my mouth: it shall not return unto me void, but it shall accomplish that which I please, and it shall prosper in the thing whereto I sent it.

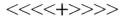

Da Vinci illustrated on canvas the divine sequence of heaven's "Code of Order;" **Logos and Rhema**.

John the Baptist…
Da Vinci and the "Bacchus" Connection

The Biblical Mystery of John The Baptist
1510 – 1515
oil on wood 177 x 115 cm

Decoding…..

It has been stated that Da Vinci's painting of John the Baptist is difficult to interpret because it illustrates attributes of John the Baptist linking and overlaying inferences of Bacchus, the god of wine. The painting mysteriously equates the **god of wine** with John the Baptist, who was the priestly descendant of Aaron

The reason why the painting of John the Baptist is so difficult to interpret is because it has been **overlaid** with two *thoughts* of ancient wisdom.

This painting has the Biblical visual wisdom of the Bible's forerunner before salvation; the Lord's cousin John the Baptist; however, this painting also has the **pre-existing** wisdom of Bacchus, the earth's **false** god of wine; familiar spirits among us from heaven's eviction, which gained authority after SIN.

John the Baptist…
Da Vinci and the "Bacchus" Connection

Decoding…….

The perspective of the painting is that John the Baptist is the forerunner of the **future** *(forerunner of the lamb of God)*, but the ancient attributes of Bacchus the god of wine is the **pre-existing past** of the fallen spirits of Lucifer; before Lucifer's eviction, all souls were with God; all of heaven's hosts were with God.

In order to understand the overlaid interpretation, we must go back to the knowledge of the archangel Lucifer's overthrow from heaven. The overthrow of Lucifer has a direct correlation with Da Vinci's perspectives and the Renaissance Era's knowledge of creationism, and gods of the earth, and the salvation directives.

When Lucifer was cut to the ground, *Isaiah 14:12*, he was **evicted** from heaven with a massive entourage of fallen angels; a **cataclysmic overthrow of spirits**. One third (1/3) of heaven was cut to the realm of the earth and into the 2nd heaven; **pre-existing** Biblical wisdom. Lucifer and his angels had dominion of the earth before **Adam**, but Lucifer a.k.a Satan has systematically gained false authority and false dominion thru the quagmire of religions and mankind's agreed approval. The universe only has one truth……..; ONE GOD.

John the Baptist…
Da Vinci and the "Bacchus" Connection

Decoding…….

In the painting, John the Baptist's gestures with his fingers also equate to the fallen earth (*pointed left index finger to the ground*). But the *pointed index finger to the right,* alludes to the pending blessings and salvation which cometh from the east; Post-Malachi. Da Vinci illustrates the message in the wilderness; "the Lamb of God cometh to the **fallen earth**; salvation is nigh".

In the Garden of Eden…… EVE, mentally agreed with a living, breathing serpent; it is not rocket science to comprehend that One-Third of God's souls are on the earth, ***fallen angels***, deceitfully and spiritually indoctrinating themselves as gods; this is the science roots of idolatry and paganism. It is not rocket science that One-Third of heaven was struck to the ground. Theses familiar spirits (Leviticus 19:31) gained supernatural powers on the earth when Eve agreed with the serpent in the Garden of Eden. The serpent already had **dormant** spiritual residence on the earth due to the Remnants of Lucifer's forced overthrow; these fallen angels are now demons, known today as Lucifer's entourage of iniquity. Hence, Biblically, all worship of false gods are of the origin of Lucifer's Eviction.

John the Baptist…
Da Vinci and the "Bacchus" Connection

Decoding…….

The mathematical equation of these fallen angels is

33.333333333 (percent) this same equation was sent for salvation in the Birth of Jesus. There again, these fallen angels were catastrophically discarded on the earth, devoid of heaven's powers. However, after Eve and Adam's disobedience to God, these demons gain authority of the mind of man; **(the spiritual battle of the mind).** This is the rooted realm and dimensions of our modern day witches, soothsayers, television mediums, and psychics. Biblically, all forms of witchcraft feed and rely on this origin inter-mixture of Adam and Eve's Pandora's Agreement **coupled** with the pre-existence of Lucifer's overthrow on the earth. One must remember that evil pre-existed **before** Adam, within the "Tree of the Knowledge of Good and Evil"; Genesis 2:17.

These fallen angels, are the reason why ancient Egypt and the Greeks and Romans had a different god for everyday of the calendar year; <u>One-Third</u> of heaven's fallen angels had deceived the dominion of the earth, and fermented spiritual authority within God's splendor; nature itself. Before Eve, the serpents on the earth did not have AUTHORITATIVE TITLES in nature.

John the Baptist…
Da Vinci and the "Bacchus" Connection

Decoding…….

In the Renaissance Era, it was **common** Biblical knowledge that one-third of these fallen spirits live among us on the earth. This is why spiritual history has thousands of false gods within the properties of God's creations, because these fallen spirits dominate and claim authority in nature per mankind's beliefs.

Throughout spiritual history, **mankind has given authority** to fallen spirits residing with nature, such as the god of rain, the goddess of fruits, the goddess of flowers, the god of thunder, the goddess of love, the goddess Diana of Ephesians, the god of wine, etc., etcetera., etcetera……all, <u>all</u>, **<u>all</u>**, are of the origin of God's overthrow of Lucifer

In Da Vinci's painting, Bacchus, the god of wine, is a **<u>fallen spirit</u>** on the earth; all **<u>false gods</u>** such as Bacchus have earthly authority. Leonardo da Vinci painting illustrates the conjugation of the **<u>ever present</u>** physics of the remnants of God and Lucifer's war of heaven. The image of John the Baptist is transparently transfigured with a fallen spirit called Bacchus; the painting simply has a mutation of the ancient **<u>FALSE</u>** god of wine.

John the Baptist…
Da Vinci and the "Bacchus" Connection

Decoding…….

Da Vinci meshed the divine authority of the forerunner and a conglomerate of the creation factors of genesis, false gods on the earth, and salvation nigh. Leonardo condensed an **overlaid messaging technique** of the Renaissance Biblical wisdom.

Leonardo da Vinci had a master comprehension of the spiritual realm. The Renaissance Era in general understood salvation's authority and the false spirits of gods that dwell on the earth, from the origin of Lucifer's eviction for inequity.

*Prideful and jealous Lucifer who proclaimed that he will exalt himself above God; but only with the **choice** of mankind renders his success.*

.

Leonardo da Vinci's painting of John the Baptist captures the Baptist in the Post-Malachi realm; hence, cursed is the ground, Genesis 3:18. John the Baptist was more than a prophet; he was sent from heaven as the forerunner in the fallen earth; he was filled with the Holy Ghost from his mother's womb.

DECODING...

Lady with an Ermine

Leonardo da Vinci's **Anatomy** of God's 400 Years of Silence

Prelude:
What is Da Vinci's Enigma?

Lady with an Ermine....Leonardo da Vinci's
Anatomy of God's 400 Years of Silence

Prelude: What is Da Vinci's Enigma?

Two of Leonardo da Vinci's spiritual fascinations were the facets of **the soul and the mind**. Da Vinci emphasized the status of the mind and soul in his paintings as it related to Biblical history. A few of his portraits and compositions penetrate the mystery of the divine *"Logos Thought."* Mankind, seeks divine *"thought"* from God; *"thought"* itself has two components, (components #1) is **direct** wisdom for God given through the prophets, the scriptures and the spirit, (components # 2) is the human "thought of intellect and reason," acquired from the environment and the world around us. *"Logos thought"* is direct from the 3rd heaven; however, *"thought of intellect and reason"* is from the 1st heaven. Leonardo understood God's "**Mandate of Thought**," and its origins.

Most his compositions expose the dimensions of "divine *thought*," and the progression of divine wisdom within "*thought*," also the spiritual application of "*though*t *and memory*" and the cosmological ordinances of "***logos thought;***" and the sciences thereof.

Da Vinci's portrait of the **Lady with an Ermine**, illustrates a Biblical milestone of the Logos silence of heaven's wisdom.

Lady with an Ermine....Leonardo da Vinci's Anatomy of God's 400 Years of Silence

Prelude: What is Da Vinci's Enigma?

The Riveting and Electrifying **Mystery** of the 400 Years of Silence

To further understand the profile of **God's silence against his nation** for four hundred years, Da Vinci illustrated a mesmerizing analytical portrait of how God's silence was attributed to the mind and the soul.

The Biblical years of silence were the years between the end of the Book of Malachi and the beginning of the Gospel of Matthew. In the Old Testament, before the end of Malachi, God utilized kings, prophets, covenants, and authoritative powers to spread his direct wisdom **upon the earth**. God also sent forth inspired wisdom from heaven, throughout the instruments of inspired men, priests, and through "divine thought," verbal encounters, and by way of dreams. However, God's chosen people rebelled against his Code of Order and Laws and they became severely corrupt with short term obedience and long term decay of sin, rejecting his wisdom and love. Hence, God **cut off the mind** of his nation from divine wisdom. At the end of Malachi, God became silent for four hundred (400) years.

Lady with an Ermine....Leonardo da Vinci's Anatomy of God's 400 Years of Silence

Prelude: **What is Da Vinci's Enigma?**

Continued:

The Riveting and Electrifying Mystery of the 400 Years of Silence

However, in the void of God's four hundred years of silence, the writings of the Apocrypha took hold; these were historical writings before the birth of Christ. The Apocrypha were writings inspired by men, **not** God. The **Apocrypha** were also writings of questionable authors, inspired with shortchanged "reason and intellect," but it has origins from the Maccabees'. The Greek translation for Apocrypha means *"hidden and concealed."*

Of course, other components of knowledge during God's silent years were that of human **"intellect and reason and discovery,"** as in the earth's unfolding and tinkering civilizations, also the quests of the sciences, and man's thirst for power and lust.

Lady with an Ermine….Leonardo da Vinci's
Anatomy of God's 400 Years of Silence

Prelude: What is Da Vinci's Enigma?

Continued:
The Riveting and Electrifying **Mystery** of the 400 Years of Silence

In the fullness of time, the **Silence Years** *were broken with the* **Angel Gabriel** *in the New Testament, announced to the priest Zacharias that his wife Elisabeth will give birth to a son and the child will be filled with the Holy Ghost from the mother's womb; hence, John the Baptist, the forerunner.*

The **Angel Gabriel** *in the presence of God, again broke the silence when he announced to the Virgin Mary that she will conceive a Son to be called Jesus, the Son of the Highest.*

Leonardo da Vinci's
Anatomy of God's 400 Years of Silence

Lady with an Ermine
(Cecilia Gallerani) 1483 – 1490
Oil on walnut 54.8 x 40.3 CM

Decoding…..The Mistress & The Weasel

A Biblical Allegory……

The <u>Lady with an Ermine</u> illustrates Leonardo da Vinci's visual anatomy of God's FOUR HUNDRED years of silence; at the end of Malachi. The Lady with an "Ermine" portrays this Biblical <u>Time Capsule</u> on canvas when God closed the mind of mankind from his wisdom.

This portraiture analogously and figuratively captures the physics of how God **"<u>deleted</u>"** the mind, (*omission of his divine wisdom*), during the four hundred years of silence. For centuries, Leonardo da Vinci has been characterized to be extremely enigmatic and ambiguous with many of his key works of art; the reason being that Da Vinci's interpretations transcends the normal perspective of the visual and tangible **<u>obvious</u>** and **<u>obviousness</u>**. The dominant factors and understanding of Da Vinci's compositions and portraits are directly attributed to sequences and turning points of Biblical history and mileposts.

Page 256
Leonardo da Vinci's
Anatomy of God's 400 Years of Silence

Decoding…..The Mistress & The Weasel

*Mistress Cecilia Gallerani is a Biblical **Allegory; Encoded.***

This portraiture is weighed in as the mistress of Duke Ludovico il Moro, the Lady Cecilia Gallerani. In this mystery, Da Vinci, visually stereotyped and disguised Mistress Cecilia Gallerani within the Biblical time frame of the end of the Book of Malachi; the crucial event when God was outraged at his people, and disgusted at their wicked ways and their overwhelming rebellion. Mistress Gallerani is Da Vinci's Biblical time capsule on canvas; Da Vinci illustrates the state and status of the mind during the 400 years of **wisdom's blackout** from heaven.

This painting in essence was not to grace the image and beauty of Ludovico il Moro's Mistress, Miss Gallerani, but to portray the feminine exterior façade of a period in time when **God shut *wisdom* down from the mind**. God severed, *cut,* all communications with his people for four hundred years (400 years). The portrait illustrates the enigmatic cloak and **visual** trappings of the mind severed from the Logos in the silent years after Malachi.

Leonardo da Vinci's
Anatomy of God's 400 Years of Silence

Decoding…..The Mistress & The Weasel

*Mistress Cecilia Gallerani is a Biblical **Allegory***

Unfortunately, Mistress Cecilia Gallerani was just a physical **PROP** to portray the vesturing and anatomy, and posturing of the visual logistics of Israel's four hundred years of silence; in essence, the portraiture of Mistress Gallerani was brilliantly and artistically flanked with the visual disciplines that confounded and shutdown the mind and soul from the whereabouts of God, and the wisdom of God, and knowledge of God. It was a period in time, between the Old Testament and New Testament when God turned his back on his chosen people for their evil ways, unrighteousness.

Leonardo da Vinci portrayed the Mistress Cecilia Gallerani in the sin profile and anatomical status of the Bible's 400 years of silence, wisdom cut from the mind; the model mistress is painted in a parable of God's severe penalty to his chosen race. Wisdom of God was block off **between** the time span of the Old Testament and the New Testament; the prelude years of John the Baptist, the forerunner.

Leonardo da Vinci's
Anatomy of God's 400 Years of Silence

Decoding…..The Mistress & The Weasel

The Greek word for Ermine is Gale; it seems to be a play of words, from the name of the mistress, Gallerani; and the name for weasel, Gale; which God considers the origin of weasels unclean in the Book of Leviticus. The mistress and the weasel further lends to intrigue because the weasel is said to be the Duke Ludovico il Moro's emblem and symbol and Miss Gallerani is his possession of lust. The Lady is Encoded……

Da Vinci's Cloak of God's 400 Years of Silence; Vesture & Trappings:

(1) The **<u>double straps</u>** *around the brain of Miss Gallerani, depicts the closure of the mind; God's 400 years of silence against his people; Miss Gallerani wears two straps around the mind, one for each gender; although she was a Mistress, the Duke and her were still one flesh.*

(2) The black strap around her mind, (*spiritually both hemispheres of the brain*), depicts the closure of wisdom. The double bands of restraints, which encircle her skull and forehead are spiritually symbolic of the lack of wisdom from God. Also, it visually exposes her spiritual status as a negative.

Page 259
Leonardo da Vinci's
Anatomy of God's 400 Years of Silence

Decoding.......The Lady is Encoded

Da Vinci's Cloak of God's 400 Years of Silence;
Vesture & Trappings:

(3) Gallerani's hair, appears wrapped and fused upon her ears, devoid of the glory of angels. Her hair mutes the hearing senses and encompasses and strangles her throat; as the long braid on her back is aligned with her spine. Hence, her hair is divided through the left and the right hemisphere of her mind, a metaphor of the crossroads of the two Testaments of the Bible.

(4) Gallerani's black beaded necklace, yokes her neck. How does the Bible describe the unwillingness to submit to God? *Isaiah 48:4...Because I knew that thou art obstinate, and they neck is an iron sinew, and thy brow brass; bondage.*

(5) Gallerani's right hand **enumerates** the Four Hundred years of silence. Her right hand on the weasel, *the Ermine*, **denotes four fingers**; each finger mathematically represents **ONE HUNDRED** years, which totals to **FOUR HUNDRED** years of punishment for the evil deeds of God's chosen people. Gallerani's index finger on the Ermine, accentuates the gravity of sin; it is further encoded with her caress of the unclean weasel.

Leonardo da Vinci's
Anatomy of God's 400 Years of Silence

Decoding…….

Da Vinci's Cloak of God's 400 Years of Silence;
Vesture & Trappings:

(6) On Gallerani's left sleeve, the pleated slit in her garment is indicative of the blood of Christ concealed; and pending. The weasel's right paw rests on the blood that cometh nigh; salvation thereof. The focal point of the garment's sleeve, illustrates the metaphorical blood concealed; the mandate of God.

(7) The mistress and the weasel both look attentively towards the EAST; waiting for the future release of the mind's spiritual incarceration; God's punishment to his people for rebellion.

The allegorical portrait also illustrates the persona of **<u>EVIL</u>** with the **<u>UNCLEAN</u>** starring towards the East.

Leviticus 11:29…These also shall be unclean unto you among the creeping things that creep upon the earth; <u>the</u> <u>weasel</u>, and the mouse, and the tortoise after his kind,

Leonardo da Vinci's Anatomy of God's 400 Years of Silence

Decoding.......

Da Vinci encodes Bible disciplines in many of his subject's dress code. The ornate garment and hair arrangements of Miss Gallerani depicts and projects the disciplines of a critical Biblical turning point known as the silence years after the Book of Malachi, when God imposed a spiritual blackout against his people.

In the Lady with an Ermine, Da Vinci depicted the feminine with the closure of the mind as it relates to the four hundred (400) years of silence, dormant from all of God's wisdom. Wisdom came back with John the Baptist after four hundred years. Leonardo, was illustrating the physics of the 400 years of silence upon the willing subject model of the Duke's young Mistress.

In his spiritual works of Art, Da Vinci **extracted the status of the soul,** first. Leonardo's approach to the canvas was to first concentrate on the countenance of the soul; the soul directs the outer façade of the human being; flesh. Leonardo knew that only the soul was the life, only the soul is the breath, and only the soul navigates the senses and the mind of mankind.

Page 262
Leonardo da Vinci's
Anatomy of God's 400 Years of Silence

Most, if not all, of Da Vinci's spiritual paintings primarily encode the art of transfiguration of the spiritual status and posture, or the spiritual stance of the person's soul in the equation of good **verses** evil **verses** tormented. This is why most of Leonardo's portraits and other Renaissance Arts are so mysterious and captivating because the first intent of the artist was to capture on canvas the **status of the subject's soul**; the format or template of a soul; for example:

Was the soul pending the future?
Reference: John the Baptist. 1513 – 1516

Was the soul without wisdom?
Reference: Lady with an Ermine, 1483-1490

Was the soul generational?
Reference: The Virgin & Child and St. Anne

Was the soul in torment?
Reference: St Jerome in the Wilderness, 1479-1481

Was Lucifer's music grounded?
Reference: Portrait of a Musician, ca 1490

Were the souls still under-the-law, in the Old Testament?
Reference: Madonna & Child with a **Pomegranate**, ca. 1470

Were the souls under grace in the New Testament?
Reference: Madonna & Child with a **Carnation**; ca. 1473-1476

Leonardo da Vinci's Anatomy of God's 400 Years of Silence

Leonardo da Vinci and many other Renaissance Artists illustrated various authorities of Scripture on Canvas; they also extracted and transfigured on canvas the subject's spiritual **position with evil** or their spiritual **position with virtue and goodness**. The soul was the primary criteria of the artist and his brush; the contents of the subject's soul on canvas was observed, first. In other portraits and paintings, Da Vinci depicted the metaphors of the Biblical events and milestones.

Most of the emphasis and accents of authorities in the fashioned clothing, garments, and trappings of accessories were to capture the dynamics of the exterior persona of the subject's Biblical disciples, merits and demerits. Da Vinci's Biblical knowledge and powers of observation gave him a command wisdom of God **with** science; creationism.

Beyond the portrait revelations of **The Lady with an Ermine**, the genius, Leonardo da Vinci also had a cosmic understanding of the universe and the creator, and its **command infrastructure** which he encoded in another <u>dynamic composite sketch</u> called the <u>Uomo Universale</u>; and its secrets thereof.

Page 264
Leonardo da Vinci's
Anatomy of God's 400 Years of Silence

The following are some Renaissance portraits that illustrate the **authority of the soul** by way of their vestures, fashioned clothing, loose garments, and accessories of emblems, jewels, stones, ornate headdress, braids and bands.

Virtue:
Da Vinci Portrait of Ginevra de Benci

Quamire of Mystisium:
Botticelli's Portrait of Simonetta Vespucci

Authority of Rulers:
Ercole de Roberti Portrait of Ruler of Bologna and his wife

Closure of Wisdom:
Da Vinci Portrait of Lady with an Ermine

The Biblical Feminine Factors..."*for the man is not of the woman; but the woman of the man*"

The Biblical Mystery of the <u>Three</u> Mary (s) at the Foot of the Cross of Jesus

Due to the deception of the alleged marriage of Jesus and Mary Magdalene in Dan Brown's novel "The Da Vinci Code," it is note worthy to reveal how God blessed each of the three Mary (s) in their own separate spiritual realm.

The three Mary (s) at the foot of the cross have separate spiritual merits and equations.

- 1- Mary, the Mother of Jesus
- 2- Mary, the sister of the Virgin Mary, and wife of Cleophas
- 3- Mary Magdalene, the repented woman and servant of the Lord.

The three Mary (s) at the foot of the Cross at Calvary have a unique distinction and spiritual status in the realm of heaven and the earth's Spiritual War.

The Biblical Feminine Factors…"*for the man is not of the woman; but the woman of the man*"

DECODING…The Virgin Mary

The Biblical Mystery of the <u>Three</u> *Mary (s) at the Foot of the Cross of Jesus*

<u>Mary the Mother of Jesus</u>
Mary No.1..Mandate of the **<u>Third Heaven;</u>**
Equation: Spiritual numeric is of NINE (9).

Mary, the Mother of Jesus was mandated in the third (3) heaven; the realm of the Godhead. She is the divine spoken "HOLY ORDER" of the **<u>Third (3) Jerusalem,</u>** the God of the Most High.

Matthew 1:17,18, 19,20,21…kjv
So all the generations from Abraham to David are fourteen generations; and from David until the carrying away into Babylon are fourteen generations; and from the carrying away into Babylon unto Christ are fourteen generations. 18 Now the birth of Jesus Christ was on this wise:

The Biblical Feminine Factors…*"for the man is not of the woman; but the woman of the man"*

DECODING…The Virgin Mary
Matthew 1:17,18,19,20,21…continued
When as his mother Mary was espoused to Joseph, before they came together, she was found with child of the Holy Ghost. 19 Then Joseph her husband, being a just man, and not willing to make her a public example, was minded to put her away privily. 20 But while he thought on these things, behold, the angel of the Lord appeared unto him in a dream, saying, Joseph, thou son of David, fear not to take unto thee Mary thy wife: for that which is conceived in her is of the Holy Ghost. 21 And she shall bring forth a son, and thou shalt call his name JESUS: for he shall save his people from their sins.

Mary, the mother of Jesus was the divine, sacred woman, mandated by God to bring forth the spoken Word of God, the savior from her virgin womb for humanity's salvation. The Virgin Mary's divine marriage was pre-destined and mandated, **BEFORE-THE-LAW.**

Numerical Order:

The Virgin Mary is the only woman on the face of the earth with a spiritual numeric of **NINE**; because her origins are from the third (3) Heaven; 3rd Jerusalem, and her womb carried the conception of the Holy Spirit.

The Biblical Feminine Factors…"*for the man is not of the woman; but the woman of the man*"

DECODING…Mary the Aunt of Jesus

The Biblical Mystery of the <u>Three</u> Mary (s) at the Foot of the Cross of Jesus

Mary, the Wife of Cleopas
Mary No. 2…Blessed Under-the-law; the <u>**Second Heaven;**</u> *2nd Jerusalem*

Equation: Spiritual numeric is of seven (7)

Mary, the wife of Cleophas, was the sister of the Virgin Mary; hence, Aunt of Jesus. This Mary was the mother of James the less and Joses. She is referred as the "other Mary" who was present with Mary Magdalene at the burial of Jesus; she was also one of those who went in the morning of the first day of the week to anoint the body of Jesus and became one of the first witnesses of the resurrection.

The Biblical Feminine Factors…"*for the man is not of the woman; but the woman of the man*"

DECODING…Mary the Aunt of Jesus

This Mary's divine marriage was under-the-law in the realm of the Second Heaven; i.e., 2nd Jerusalem. Her marriage was in **ONENESS UNDER-THE-LAW.**

Did Satan Have Powers of Authority to Enter Into the Second Heaven?

YES, INDEED.
Matthew 4:8,9…Again, the devil taketh him up into an exceeding high mountain, and showeth him all the Kingdoms of the world, and the glory of them; 9 And saith unto him, All these things will I give thee, if thou wilt fall down and worship me.

Numerical Order:

Mary, the sister of the Virgin Mary, and wife of Cleophas, of course, is afar from her sister the Virgin Mary; this Mary's spiritual numeric was a SEVEN (7), because her **WOMB** borne children of a man, in the fallen earth, and under the auspices of THE LAW.

The Biblical Feminine Factors…"*for the man is not of the woman; but the woman of the man*"

DECODING…Mary the Aunt of Jesus

Reference Scriptures:

Matthew 27:56…kjv

Among which was Mary Magdalene, and Mary the mother of James and Joses, and the mother of Zebedee's children.

Matthew 27:61…kjv

And there was Mary Magdalene, and the other Mary, sitting over against the sepulchre.

Matthew 28:1…kjv

In the end of the Sabbath, as it began to dawn toward the first day of the week, came Mary Magdalene and the other Mary to see the sepulchre.

Mark 15:40…kjv

There were also women looking on afar off: among whom was Mary Magdalene, and Mary the mother of James the less and of Joses, and Salome;

The Biblical Feminine Factors…*"for the man is not of the woman; but the woman of the man"*

DECODING…Mary the Aunt of Jesus

Mark 15:47…And Mary Magdalene and Mary the mother of Joses beheld where he was laid.

Mark 16:1…kjv
And when the Sabbath was past, Mary Magdalene, and Mary the mother of James, and Salome, had bought sweet spices, that they might come and anoint him.

John 19:25…kjv
Now there stood by the cross of Jesus his mother, and his mother's sister, Mary the wife of Cleophas, and Mary Magdalene.

Matthew 4:8…Again, the devil taketh him up into an exceeding high mountain, and showeth him all the kingdoms of the world, and the glory of them; 9 And saith unto him, All these things will I give thee, if thou wilt fall down and worship me.

The Biblical Feminine Factors…"*for the man is not of the woman; but the woman of the man*"

DECODING…Mary of Magdala

The Biblical Mystery of the <u>Three</u> Mary (s) at the Foot of the Cross of Jesus

Mary Magdalene:
Mary No. 3…Saved in the Crossroads of Law and Grace; the *First Heaven*

Equation: Spiritual numeric **before Jesus,** she was a SIX (6)

After the mercy of Jesus, her spiritual numeric was a SEVEN (7).

Mary Magdalene was the woman at the crossroad of heaven's war. Unlike, <u>Mary, the mother of Jesus</u> and <u>Mary, the wife of Cleophas</u>. Evidently and under-the-law, Mary Magdalene was out of the **"WILL"** of God. She was possessed by seven demons, evidence of a generational curse.

The Biblical Feminine Factors..."*for the man is not of the woman; but the woman of the man*"

DECODING...Mary of Magdala

Mary Magdalene was the woman in the crossroads of Law and Grace; a woman saved personally by **The LORD of LORDS** *before the shedding of his blood, and before the pivotal arrival of the Holy Spirit. Evidently, she was a tormented woman without a husband and family;* existing in the daily realm of spiritual war. Before repentance, she was the composite of a tormented feminine, suffering in the crossroads of the Old Testament.

Numerical Order:

Mary Magdalene, also known as, Mary of Magdala, a town on the western shore of the Lake of Tiberias. Mary Magdalene was at the crossroads of Law and Grace. Without the mercy and grace of her deliverer, the Lord Jesus, the demons the entered into her body would have tormented her soul perpetually.

The Biblical Feminine Factors…*"for the man is not of the woman; but the woman of the man"*

DECODING…Mary of Magdala

Under-the-Law, Mary Magdalene's spiritual numeric was a six **BEFORE** the Lord Jesus cast out her seven demons. Mary Magdalene's spiritual numeric became a seven ***AFTER*** she followed in the footsteps of the Lord; under-the-law.

Before she encountered the grace and mercy of the Lord Jesus, Mary Magdalene was severely tormented through the daily Spiritual War in the First Heaven; crossroads of the 1st Jerusalem.

Does Satan Have Authoritative Powers in the First Heaven? YES, INDEED.

Matthew 4:3,4,5,6,7…And when the tempter came o him, he said, If thou be the Son of God, command that these stones be made bread. 4 But he answered and said, It is written, Man shall not live by bread alone, but by every word that proceedeth out of the mouth of God. 5 Then the Devil taketh him up into the holy city, and setteth him on a pinnacle of the temple, 6 And saith unto him, If thou be the Son of God, cast thyself down: for it is written, He shall give his angels charge concerning thee: and in their hands they shall bear thee up, lest at any time thou dash thy foot against a stone. 7 Jesus said unto him, It is written again, Thou shalt not tempt the Lord thy God.

The Biblical Feminine Factors..."*for the man is not of the woman; but the woman of the man*"

DECODING...Mary of Magdala

Repeat Reference Scriptures:

Matthew 27:56, Matthew 27:61, Matthew 28:1, Mark 15:40, Mark 15:47, Mark 16:1, John 19:25

Matthew 28:5...kjv
And the angel answered and said unto the women, Fear not ye: for I know that ye seek Jesus, which was crucified.

Mark 15:41...kjv
(Who also, when he was in Galilee, followed him, and ministered unto him;) and many other women which came up with him unto Jerusalem.

Luke 23:55,56...kjv
And the women also, which came with him from Galilee, followed after, and beheld the sepulchre, and how his body was laid. 56 And they returned, and prepared spices and ointments; and rested the Sabbath day according to the commandment.

Da Vinci's Self Portrait…
The Perspective Within God's Omnipresence

Decoding…..

Self Portrait
1513, ca 1513
The Last Years
Drawing: 33.2 x 21.2 cm

The Five Senses Within the Omnipresence of the Creator

*The Five Human Senses Within the <u>**Sixth Sense**</u> of the Spiritual*

The Omnipresent Factor:

Leonardo da Vinci was thoroughly fascinated by the creator of heaven and earth; he firmly understood that God was <u>**the mover and the shaker**</u> of the entire universe, as his notes infer.

In Da Vinci's Self-portrait, ca. 1513, of the Last Years, he portrays this portrait with very, very, minimal substance of the physical realm, physical flesh, skin, and body.

Da Vinci's Self Portrait…
The Perspective Within God's Omnipresence

Decoding…..

Remarkably, Leonardo da Vinci dilutes his facial likeness within the physics of **empty space**; he uses the fullness of invisible depth to ingrain and surround his own facial perspective within the spiritual omnipresence of God; his subtle likeness <u>WITHIN</u> the spiritual <u>WITHIN</u>. Da Vinci recesses his countenance in a dramatic subliminal and spiritual dimension, rendering texture to the **emptiness of space**; God's breath and omnipresence.

In essence, Da Vinci, delineates his transparent facial likeness in the inner realm of space and time; the omnipresence of God.

This portrait spiritually illustrates and commands the **FIVE SENSES** of mankind; the sketch exteriorizes the senses of SIGHT, SMELL, TASTE, HEARING, and TOUCH, all of which are recessed and surrounded within nothingness in the sketch. This masterpiece envelops the five principle human features that orchestrate mankind's FIVE SENSES, within the spiritual **SIXTH SENSE** of God's ever-present physics.

Leonardo da Vinci embedded his own **FIVE SENSES** in the fabric of nothingness.

Da Vinci's Self Portrait…
The Perspective Within God's Omnipresence

Decoding…..

This self portrait depicts the **EYES** which are the windows of heaven and the witnesses of good and evil on the earth. Next is the nose, the NOSTRILS, which take in the breath of life and perceives the sense of **SMELL**. The senses of **HEARING AND TOUCH** in the portrait are united with the association of the long hair, which fades in the void of space.

……Last but not least, Da Vinci gives great emphasis to the mouth. The mouth that of which houses the sense of **TASTE**, and it houses the **tongue**, the spiritual vehicle of death or life. *Proverbs 18:21…Death and life are in the power of the tongue: and they that love it shall eat the fruit thereof.*

The tongue savors all of the earth's fruited morsels and delicacies of human sustenance; it also directs the waters of life into the body……**but**, out of all the components of the human senses the **tongue** is the deadliest. Satan holds God accountable for all demerits of the **tongue**. In the self-portrait, Da Vinci, has a toughened and transcendental demeanor of the eyes and mouth that are shutdown and withdrawn from the world.

Page 279
Da Vinci's Self Portrait…
The Perspective Within God's Omnipresence

The Mouth Shelters the Tongue

The Tongue;
Author of Poem - Unknown

"The boneless tongue so small and weak
Can crush and kill, " declared the <u>Greek</u>;

"The tongue destroys a greater horde,"
The <u>Turk</u> asserts, "than does the sword."

The <u>Persian</u> proverb wisely saith,
"A lengthy tongue---an early death,"
Or Sometimes takes this form instead,
"Don't let your tongue cut off your head."

"The tongue can speak a word, whose speed,"
Says the <u>Chinese</u>, "outstrips the steed,"
While <u>Arab</u> sages this impart:
"The tongue's great storehouse is the Heart,"

From <u>Hebrew</u> with the maxim sprung:
"though feet may slip, ne'er let the tongue;"
The <u>sacred writer crowns</u> the whole:
"Who keeps his tongue, doth keep his soul."

Da Vinci's Self Portrait…
The Perspective Within God's Omnipresence

Decoding…..

The power of the tongue can be extremely destructive, because everything, everything that is spoken by man is taken into account in heaven; spiritually it is believed that Da Vinci was more of an introvert because of the tongue's power to destroy itself; hence, **silence is Golden.** As a child Leonardo da Vinci was keen to all the senses, physically and spiritually, he was the only genius in history that transcended **God** above science.

Da Vinci even had the profound wisdom of the spiritual intricacies of the human mind, because he thoroughly understood that God is the physics of the **Logos** who reins the "**thoughts**" of the mind towards the speech of **tongue**. God is the curator of the mind and the memory; God observes, then navigates the mind in **compliance with the heart** and then the **tongue**.
Jeremiah 17:9…The heart is deceitful above all things, and desperately wicked: who can know it?

*……In summary the ancients knew the blessing and curses of the **tongue**. The penalties of the tongue are silent to the flesh but inevitably **accountable** to the soul; daily.*

What Did Leonardo Da Vinci Know…
about the Universe and God?

What Did Da Vinci Know?

Leonardo da Vinci knew that in the expanse of our Solar System, the terrestrial and the celestial planets are aligned with perfect sovereign "TIME;" the rotations of "TIME" itself were pre-destined by God. Hence, our solar system is… an aligned cosmic **CLOCK**; it is the celestial clock of the earth's precise and perfect DIVINE ORDER within heaven's eternal LAWS.

Da Vinci also understood that God is the controlling and dominant force of the universe; he fully comprehended and illustrated the origin physics of "**divine thought**" within the dynamics of creationism and the salvation plans for the human soul. ……..Biblically and scientifically, the greatest err in the history of human "thought and reason," is that a person's fate is believed to be happenstance.

1st Corinthians 15:40…There are also celestial bodies, and bodies terrestrial: but the glory of the celestial is one, and the glory of the terrestrial is another. There is one glory of the sun, and another glory of the moon, and another glory of the stars: for one star differeth from another star in glory;… KJV